Coming Out of
The Dark

Anna Gray

BOOKHUB®
PUBLISHING GROUP

Published by Book Hub Publishing
Interior formatting by Dorothy Dreyer
For further information re national & international distribution
www.bookhubpublishing.com info@bookhubpublishing.com
Twitter: @BookHubPublish Insta: @bookhub_publishing

Anna Gray may be booked to speak or present on the themes of her book by
contacting www.bookhubpublishing.com at 00 353 91 846953

Printed in the Republic of Ireland
First Edition 2018
ISBN 978-1-9998951-6-7

Dedication

This book is dedicated to my incredible partner Paul. Without you, I know I would not have seen this through. Thank you for every word of love, support and strength throughout this process. Thank you for listening to me in every panicked conversation I started, every fearful ramble I had and every doubt I expressed whilst writing this. You have been my rock, my sanctuary and my place I call 'home'. I love you x

Acknowledgements

A huge thanks to Book Hub Publishing for their support and for creating this opportunity for me to publish a book about my life. Thank you to everyone who has worked hard on my behalf to make it possible.

Thank you to all my amazing family members who have championed me during this last year. Your belief in me and your encouragement during this process have meant the world.

INTRODUCTION

Hello and thank you for choosing to read my book. My name is Anna Gray. I am a 37-year-old woman from Belfast and this is my story of Transformation. I have lived in Belfast for most of my life, spending some time living in Dublin with my family when I was younger and a little time living in Scotland too. It was important to me that this book is more than *just* a story of my life, because the issues that I write about throughout it are bigger than me and touch so many people's lives every day. I wanted to offer my story and to address some of these larger issues from the perspective of what I have learned about them, both personally and professionally. Throughout my book, I will address topics such as bullying, self-harm, trichotillomania, alcohol abuse, intimate partner relationship violence, counselling and healing practices to name but some.

My hope is that in reading about my life, you will come to know that transformation is possible for you and for the people you love and hold dear to you. I sincerely hope that my own experiences will speak to you somehow and, at the very least, offer some kind of comfort and inspiration to you. With an open heart, I will share with you an honest account of my own struggles and pain and how I overcame them. I don't account for everything that ever happened in my life, for every year that passed or for every lesson learned – to do so would take a lot more than one book. However, the major and important landmarks, as I see them, are there and they are all true for me and fairly represented.

I now work as a counsellor and life coach with people every day that are experiencing some of the same struggles that I did, in one form or another. There was a time when that seemed like an unachievable dream, as my life was difficult and full of indescribable and secret pain. I was convinced that it would always be like that for me and that there was something fundamentally wrong with me, something that would never heal. I don't claim to have experienced or understand everything that people go through, there is some horrific and down right unfair circumstances that people are dealing with out there, things I hope I never come to have personal experience with. However, I've had my fair share and then some. Some self-inflicted, some inflicted by others. It's irrelevant to me either way, as pain is pain. I have been to what felt like the depths of hell and I have returned from the mountain with a message. It's one of hope.

I deeply desired to write this book for a number of years, but something inside me always knew that when the time was right, I would be shown very clearly the time was right and that the timing would be perfect. I trusted that and, thank goodness, it all beautifully fell into place.

It was November 2017 when I was sitting at my desk in Belfast and I looked up at the sky and asked for help. I felt it was time that I was ready to write, although the prospect terrified me. I knew I didn't have the first clue about how to write a book, never mind what followed with sending it to Publishers and all the horror stories I had heard of 100 rejection letters arriving at once. You will see as my story progresses that I developed a strong belief of there being more to life than meets the eye and that we are helped by the Universe, if only we ask and take notice of that help. I didn't always believe that so it's not meant as a flippant comment, it was a hard-earned feeling of being supported by something other than my own strength of will.

As I sat at my desk with my heart pounding, I spoke silently to myself;

"Please somebody help me with this, I am feeling the urge to write now, it's time for me to share my story. Bring me the right people, circumstances and Publisher to get this message out there in the right way. I want to do it with support, with the backing of an amazing Company, with motivated and inspiring people who will believe in what I want to say. Thank you."

That was it. That's all I said, but I said it with such conviction and heart that I knew it was heard. I truly believe and have learned from experience that we have to ask for help, we have to work hand in hand with the Universe. We have to co-create. I sent my intention out there and I trusted 100% that what I had sent out would attract the right opportunity for me. Intention is nothing without action and my action was asking for direction and beginning to write regardless of how long it took for my intentions to manifest results.

As it turned out, I didn't have to wait that long. Two weeks in fact. I noticed a friend request from a woman I had no connections with, any mutual friends or previous interactions. Her name is Aine Lisa McAuley Crosse. As I looked at her profile, I spotted that she had listed Book Hub Publishing in Galway as her workplace. A little shiver went up my spine as I wondered if this was my first sign. I sent her a message and discovered she had just published her own book with them called 'Angels, Autism, Mitochondrial and Me'. A fantastic book that I really recommend reading. A few messages went back and forth between us and then came the one that clinched it for me;

"Anna, I don't know what made me want to connect with you, I just kept getting the feeling to ask you if you had ever wanted to write your own book? I have never contacted someone I don't know before but I felt compelled to ask you that."

I replied quickly saying I had been thinking of it. She passed me the name and number of the MD of Book Hub Publishing, Dr. Niall McElwee and encouraged me to contact him.

I shook with energy for the rest of the day, half with utter shock and half with a sense of excitement I had never felt before. It took me a few days to let it sink in and to get up the courage to make contact. I'm utterly convinced I sounded like a blubbering wreck when I made the first phone call to Niall, asking him if I could send him over some material I had written. Praise be his patience and sensitivity with me!

I knew straight away that this was big for me; I could feel the gravity of following this through and what it would mean for me. I was under no illusions, whatsoever, that I would need to be sharing the truth and nothing but the truth. I knew I couldn't dip my toe into the deep end of my life and write only what I wanted people to hear. That's a scary realisation and I often felt waves of fear swallowing me. There was, and still a conviction in my heart however, to go all in, to share warts and all. There were lots of moments of deep breathing and panicked phone calls to friends to deal with before the first meeting.

At my first meeting in Galway, I was 100% sure that I wanted to do this, I trusted what I was hearing and the support and guidance I got from the offset really surpassed any normal expectations. I really had got what I had asked for that day at my desk, a professional and motivated publishing company who believed in me and what I had to say. Plus, as a bonus, a sense of humour was welcomed and championed – a must for me! To say I felt and still feel blessed and grateful would be a huge understatement.

Sitting over coffee at our meeting, I knew I had to be ready, to come out of the dark, to tell my life as it really was and is, to step into the light. There's a big difference you see, in knowing it all inside and feeling transformed and actually telling people about it, allowing people into the dirty corners of my life that have remained hidden and covered in spiders' webs. I could take the leap or not, it was in my hands. I honestly felt I was standing on the edge of a cliff. I knew if I didn't fully invest myself in this that I would regret it for the rest of my life. So I trusted and I jumped. And I'm so glad I did.

The years of pain, abuse, guilt, shame and ultimate healing and transformation are laid out in the pages that follow. There have been many layers of fears to work through to get them onto paper, fear of judgement, of shocking the people who know me – the ultimate fear of being 'seen' in my entirety. No matter what, it's worth it, for you to be able to read this and for the possibility of it helping someone else. Yes, it is a story about me, but it's one that so many people may resonate with and I trust that it will reach the people who need to read it.

I hope you enjoy reading it as much as I have enjoyed writing it, it truly has been an amazing journey of self discovery and personal development.

CHAPTER 1 - FAMILY MATTERS

$\mathcal{I}$ would like to share a little with you about my family history. The stories I grew up hearing and my early experiences of my family life formed the eyes through which I first saw the world and were the foundations on which I built my sense of identity. I've always had a great love for my family and a healthy pride in the stories of my ancestors. I've seen parts of my life mirroring theirs at times and I've felt deeply connected to their histories, their personal challenges and successes included.

There's Gypsy blood in my veins, and I use the word Gypsy in the old-fashioned respectful way. It's often used as an insult these days and that's such a shame. Some of my ancestors were Travellers with Romany blood in their line from Devon in England who came to Ireland 4 generations ago. There was a wildness, a passion and a power that I was born with because of them, an ability to get-up and go at a moment's notice and start all over again. It gave me great 'bounce-back-ability' my dad once told me. I seemed to inherit both their rumoured addictive personalities and their fieriness, but also, their apparent ability to feel the Spirit World and to sense some things about the future, although unfortunately not much about my own at times! I guess we can't have it all.

Darkie was my Great Grandfather; he was a bare-knuckle boxer on the streets of Belfast. He had never been beaten apparently, which was some feat in those days around Belfast. People used to pay just to watch him fight on street corners, no matter what the weather. He was nicknamed Darkie because of his hair, it was jet black and thick and shiny in a way that made him look vaguely like a film star in the pictures I have seen of him. The stories passed down to us about him all celebrated his strength and valour. I grew up hearing of his fights and I would conjure up dreamy images of him standing under a lamppost somewhere in the heart of the City, fire in his eyes and pride in his stance. His family was very poor, I've been told, burning their wooden stairs on the open fire in the living room to try and keep warm. Belfast had many poor areas back then in the 1940's and onwards and I heard many times how it was a treat to go to the local chippy for a deep fried pig's trotter and a scoop of chips. I guess he was just making money in whatever way he could and if he got a few coins for being strong in a fight, it was more than he had before it.

Then there was Veenie, my 'crazy' Great Aunt, who I now know wasn't that crazy after all. She was just misunderstood. She had eyes as black as midnight and she said she could see Spirits and the future, but that wasn't accepted or normal in those days in the

1960's and 70's, so she was considered to be a bit strange because that made people feel safer. When we went to visit her in her later life in the 1980's, she used to serve us corned beef cut into slices and tomato sandwiches that none of us wanted to eat. There was no money at that time and it was the best she could do. I was intrigued by her uniqueness and she seemed somehow exotic and untamable to my younger self. I used to stand in her garden and wonder what it would be like to live in her house as she represented rebellion and freedom to me and a small part of me wanted to be just like her.

I have to admit a favourite story of mine about her was about a time she was so desperate for her freedom and release from the boredom and poverty of Belfast that she jumped out her bedroom window and ran off to try and get on the Liverpool boat. She was so close, she almost got there. I can nearly feel her soul soar and expand at the sight of the boat, the wind in her hair, her eyes shining with an indescribable hope. Her brother was there waiting for her, him and the rest of his Orange Order band. They marched her through the streets back home, drums beating and all. Her one chance of a new life gone. I can't even bear to imagine how that must have crushed her spirit. I recognised something within me when I heard that story and it's one I think of often. I certainly had the impulse to run away hundreds of times in my life, to find some other dream life that promised better things, a romantic notion of happiness and change that never quite came off.

My dear Granny Vera, who I still miss every day, was a source of inspiration to me growing up. She was wild and free in a way that made you love her instantly. A heart of gold and kindness in bucket fulls, her smokers-cough-come-hysterical-laugh could send me off on a giggling spree that resulted in sore stomach muscles and tears running down my face without me ever needing to know what we were actually laughing at. She lived, in her later years, in Whitby, England, beside the sea. She always had a big pork pie in her fridge and a pocket full of loose change to sneak down to the slot machines in the amusement arcade with, laughing all the way with a bag of chips in her hands. She was hilarious, telling people exactly what she thought of them, yet remaining incredibly generous and kind hearted. When she would take me and my sister for walks, we would ask where we were going and she would throw her head back in the wind and cackle loudly as she shouted 'Wherever our 'feets' takes us' over her shoulder at us as we tried to keep up with her.

She never lost her Belfast accent and it would become ever more pronounced when she was around her family. She worked in a tiny little sea front shop that sold rock candyfloss and burgers with fried onions on them. That smell still brings me back 30 years to her generous portions and sneaky free bags of chips and if I close my eyes I can still hear her infectious laugh. I loved her intensely and was truly heartbroken when she passed away in 2011.

That was on my Dad's side. Mum's side held different stories. I would sit with her in front of our old black and white TV and eagerly ask for her to tell me again about my Great Granny

Margaret, who would read the tea leaves and tell her neighbours their fortunes, when nobody had any money to pay her she asked for biscuits as a trade-off instead. Women would come and sit in her '2 up, 2 down' house and wait their turn, custard creams in their handbags and husbands waiting at home for their dinners, tutting and shaking the papers they were pretending to read when their wives eventually arrived back to get the stew on. She was from Lurgan in Northern Ireland, from a farming family who lost everything in a card game bet one night and had to move out and come to Belfast, ashamed and pretty penniless.

Great Granny Susan was believed to have been able to levitate tables with just her fingertips back in the 1940's when that kind of thing got you locked up. Curious friends would gather in her house on a Sunday night, nervously waiting to see if the rumours were true, hoping that it was at the same time as hoping it wasn't. I was never able to get definitive confirmation either way on that one, but secretly I hoped it was true as it made her so interesting to me. I saw a picture of her once in her nurse's uniform; a cold hardened face stared back at bleak eyes, a staunch pose and me. She looked like she'd had a really hard life and I felt sorry for her. It looked as if she was locked in a sense of propriety and duty somehow in that picture and I wondered if she lived that way everyday.

I never got to meet Susan, Margaret or Darkie, and sadly they have passed on now, but hearing about the ladies' 'abilities,' introduced me to the idea that there was more to life than what I was being taught in Sunday School, and maybe there was such a thing as Spirits and being able to see the future. So, from an early age, I felt there was more. I believed there was more. This made me feel different to my peers and it made me stand out in a way that was not accepted in Belfast in the 1980's. It wasn't that I ever spoke out loud about what I'd heard about the 'abilities,' I just had an air about me that was unusual for the time. On school days where we were to speak about our families, I would happily announce that I had Gypsy blood running through my veins and I could see the change that came over my friends and teachers faces, as if somehow they were a little in awe, a little judgemental and a little afraid of me all of a sudden. My immediate family and our home was a joy to be born into and the memories I share next are cherished ones full of love, some pain and in true Gray household fashion, peppered with a little humour.

When I was 6 years old my Mum Esther rushed into our living room and put on a record called 'La Bamba'. Our record player was old and dusty and an awful shade of red, but it worked and that's all we cared about at that time. The room smelt like toast, it must have been after school because she always made me toast after we had taken our long walk home over the Ormeau Bridge, past the fruit shop that she always hoped I would pick my snack from instead of the sweet shop beside it. We had that 1970's wallpaper, the colour of mustard with garish flower prints and our floor was covered in a faded brown carpet that had seen better days, but it didn't matter, we were happy. And, we were stylish.

We danced together round the room, holding hands, and we laughed as we spun in circles around our brown sofa, getting dizzy and tired. I copied the singer and sang along, even though the words were in Spanish and I didn't know what they meant. I still don't! It's one of my favourite memories of us together, her face was shining with happiness and there were no traces of the normal day-to-day stress of being a Mother of three children. My Mum rarely danced, so it felt particularly special that day.

Long brown hair and big hazel eyes, she was, and still is, an amazing woman. Growing up with her 7 siblings and no money in their house, she had learned how to cook beautifully and wholesomely and to keep an immaculate and welcoming home. Caring, loving, compassionate and dedicated as a Mother, I remember growing up feeling genuinely loved and taken care of. Kindness emanated from her, she was always ready to soothe, care for, provide for and love her family. She never seemed to get fed up of looking after us, although looking back as a Mother now myself, I'm sure she absolutely must have but just didn't want to show it. She always put everyone else first and rarely herself, her biggest pleasure was having a lovely meal out with the ones she loved. Incredibly creative, she filled our home with mosaic mirrors she cut and designed by her own hand, tables she painted and material she somehow managed to turn into beautiful bed spreads, cushions and wall hangings.

When my Dad John came home that night my Mum and I were dancing, we changed the record to 'There's a guy works down the chip shop swears he's Elvis' by Kirsty McColl. He was wearing his work suit and a crisp white shirt, as being a teacher, he always made sure he looked smart and those were the days of starched collars and tight ties. Dark brown hair and a questionable moustache that felt prickly when I kissed him goodnight were his trademarks. His black leather shoes shone with the polish I had used on them the previous Sunday night when I had asked to learn how to do it. He loved music and had more records than I could count.

He let me put my tiny feet on top of his and he held onto my hands as he tried to show me how to Jive, or to do the Twist. I'm not sure which one it was. He became, and has remained, my hero in that moment. That's one of the happiest memories of my life, I felt so safe, so loved, so full of joy and possibility and expression. Our home was always this way, a place of happy family meals, music, laughter, a million books and really bad sing-a-longs. When we were sick, as children, Dad would always bring us a different 'Mr Men' book home to read to us and add to our collection. He taught us to read a wide variety of books, to educate ourselves as much as possible and to open our minds to the world outside of our four walls. As a teacher, he held academic education as one of the most important things in life to have and it became engrained in me as I grew up that qualifications were essential for a good life.

Dad was never a believer in the afterlife or in Angels and the like, although I think my years of telling him all about my experiences might have softened him. The only time in my childhood that he said anything to me to contradict his disbelief was a story he told me about when he was in Dublin in Trinity College with Mum and they had nothing, they had literally run out of money and food and hadn't eaten in days. They were walking along the street and past a bank; a tall suited man was walking in front of them, holding a huge wad of cash in his hand. Dad told me that for the first time in his life, he asked if there was anything or anybody out there, that would they please just let the man drop one note of money, just so they could eat that day. He described to me how heartfelt his request was, how hungry they were and how much they needed it. It wasn't greed; it was pure hunger and tiredness.

As the man got into his car, one note floated out of his hands, just one. Enough to buy a meal. The note landed just at my Dad's feet as the man drove off with no time to notice he had dropped it. He said it was amazing, as if his prayer had been heard and answered immediately and he promised when he got his University grant later that month that he would give the same amount he had received to someone else who needed it. He kept his promise, giving back a million times what he received over the years in so many ways to his family and friends. He was instrumental in setting up and implementing Cross-Community education in Northern Ireland, helping to bring about real changes in the education system here for children and adults. He had and still has a real love of fair treatment and equality of opportunity, growing up in one of the most deprived areas of Belfast, he had seen many gifted and talented young people never get the chance to reach their potential due to lack of resources, opportunity and recognition.

My dear Sister, Pippa, is 7 years my elder, although we still joke about how she looks younger than me. Pippa has always been my best friend, curly auburn hair and big blue eyes, she spent her early years picking up my dummy when I threw it out of my cot, using all her pocket money to buy me Victoria Plum toys and getting no thanks for it from a toddler who didn't know how lucky she was. She put up with a lot over the years, missing lip sticks and vanishing French clothes that she had saved up to buy herself, these were the least of the ways I reminded her that she had a younger, annoying sister who wanted to copy her. She was and still is my confidant, my teacher of life, and my partner in crime. We grew together, sharing the secrets of each other's lives, crying on each other's shoulders and defending one another when the need was there. Sure, we were competitive at times in younger years as sisters can be, but underneath that was an intense love and loyalty to each other that never failed us and we have hundreds of stories of our adventures that we can laugh at hysterically now. I think my favourite one being when we shared a flat together in our 20's and it was the middle of the night, we got hungry and decided to walk to the garage at the end of our street for food. All I had clean to wear was a pair of blue tracksuit bottoms and a big jumper, finished off with pointy blue Moroccan slippers that I'd been given as a present for Christmas. Off we walked and came across a cat that was dying. Pippa, being the incredible empathic and sensitive person that she is, bent down to stroke it and cried her eyes out for a good 20 mins while I froze my toes off. Her utter devastation for an innocent animal that was in need of some love before it passed away touched me deeply and taught me so much about compassion. She simply couldn't leave an animal to die alone and she stayed with it until it passed, scooping it up in her coat and laying it under some bushes to protect it from any more cars passing. I saw into her heart that night in a way I never had before, her capacity to love the innocent and vulnerable and to feel their pain amazed me, I was humbled.

We walked back to our flat and we lay on the ground outside it for a while, staring at the stars that were so clear in the sky. We laughed and cried about life's ups and downs and we spoke at length about how this world felt too harsh and painful for us and imagined what it would be like to go back to our Gypsy ancestors ways and live freely on the land, travelling when and to where we fancied, no expectations, bills, obligations or pressures on us. We made a pact that we would find our long lost relatives who might still live that way and that we would run away with them, away from the harshness of everyday life. We didn't do it, of course, but I've not written it off yet ha-ha!

My brother Paul is 5 years older than me. He and I fought like cats and dogs when we were growing up. One of my first memories of him was of hearing how he had nearly died when he was 6; I was too young to remember it. He had fallen off a wall at the back of our house where he was playing onto a huge metal spike that pierced him from his belly button to his chest area and he became impaled on it. Our neighbour was the one who saw it and alerted my parents, who had to hold his body together on their journey to the hospital. I heard it was touch and go, by a matter of a few inches and many operations. The scar on his body ran through my family and everyone who remembered it would cry when it was mentioned. I was only a year at the time, so had no memory of it at all, but the thought of how much pain he must have been in and the sheer panic and trauma my family must have felt lived in me as if I had been there myself.

A lover of comic books, 'Doctor Who and Red Dwarf', we didn't have much in common that way. Our many childish fights often resulted in tears and frustration and famously, my broken baby fingers when my hands got shut in his bedroom door as I was trying to push my way in to steal his Atari. I've never let him forget it and often hold my crooked fingers up in his face and laugh when I want to remind him of it.

I began to see his beauty as a person as I grew up, after he was attacked randomly and beaten up in Liverpool where he was studying and he wrote to all of us in the family, expressing how deeply he loved us all. I saw a man with a genuinely decent heart, full of pure love for people and an immense desire to connect. My heart broke for him and the unfairness of what he went through. His endless humour and creative mind led him into writing poetry that I loved to read and like all of us, is a huge fan of good food, good wine and good company. I admire his dancing the most, he moves like a man made from plasticine with no bones in his body. He knows every word to every Kinks song that was ever released and will sing them, unapologetically, at the top of his voice down the phone line to me when he gets in the mood.

Dancing quite well and singing quite badly was our way of releasing stress and it connected the whole family together in a mutual sense of expressing our emotions through songs saying the things we couldn't quite put into words ourselves.

Music was how we expressed our love for each other in a way we didn't do in every day conversations. For many years, we came together around the big wooden table in the living room, records lined up in our usual order of play, beginning with happy tunes such as 'Make Me Smile' by Steve Harley & Cockney Rebel and 'The Whole Wide World' by Wreckless Eric. The adults would have a nice glass of something to raise in the air at the crucial climax points in the song and we would all punch the air, joined together in a unified sense of family tradition and shared emotion.

Later on in the night, the music would always turn to songs more associated with loss and sadness for us. Songs that were loved by ones who had passed away or ones that told stories of very real and human pain and disappointments. As soon as my Dad would jump up to change the record, before the song was really finished as he always did, and we would hear the beginnings of 'Blue Bayou' by Roy Orbison, we knew it was time to sit down and sing together in mutual maudlin, as that song was a favourite of an

Uncle who had passed away suddenly. The night would finish up with 'Desperado' by The Eagles, my Mum, sister and brother rolling their eyes and laughing as my Dad and I would sit down, close our eyes and sing every word together, occasionally sneaking a look at each other and sharing a moment of what felt like an understanding of the world and the pain of being a human in it.

We were lucky, in many ways. We had holidays that my friends' families couldn't afford because my Dad had a good job and knew how to save money. We would go to Spain and Whitby every year, eating out in beautiful restaurants that Dad had researched before we went because he loved food and wanted to educate his children about what good food was and also because we had the best conversations round the dinner table. I have many happy memories of family get-togethers followed by a few hours of singing our favourite songs and all of us ranting about how good the food was in such and such a restaurant. My parents grew up with very little and had really suffered through their University years in Dublin, in tiny flats with no heating and water running down the walls, very little food and part time jobs in bars or chip shops.

I loved my home and my family intensely and although we had our normal family arguments about who didn't tidy their room, who was stealing the remote for the TV and who didn't do their share of the dishes, there was never any real threat to our secure little unit. I was happy, knowing I was loved at home and that there was always food on the table and a comfortable warm bed to sleep in.

It was only once I began to experience the world outside of that security that I understood not everyone was as kind and loving as my family, that not everyone had my best interests at heart. I felt like I was born with a very innocent and naive heart and the cruel harsh truth of the world came as a huge shock to me at times.

I was, and still am, highly sensitive to people's moods and the atmosphere of my environment. I suppose nobody had ever heard of an 'Empath' back then, which was a shame, because if I had known what one was and how to handle it, I wouldn't have felt so out of place and vulnerable a lot of the time. An Empath is defined as 'someone with the ability to perceive the mental or emotional state of another individual' (Oxford Dictionary). That was certainly true for me growing up and it was a hard thing to live with in the days when it wasn't understood. It often meant that my emotional state was dictated by the mood of others, before I learned how to tell the difference between us. So, when things were good around me, it lifted me up. On the down side, whenever I sensed any conflict, sadness, anger or disapproval, it affected me deeply to the point of my body hurting with the pain of it. I rarely felt that at home, but one is not at home all day, every day. There came a time when I had to venture out into the world and try to find my place among others, to find a sense of identity and a place to belong.

School began beautifully for me and stayed that way until I was around 7 years old, it was full of friends and new experiences. I have memories of running around, ringlets bouncing off my shoulders, playing in sand pits and laughing on the swings. We had our sleepover parties and our birthday pass-the-parcel games and I felt part of something. I just wanted to be everyone's friend and for everyone to be mine, the world made sense to me that way, everyone being good to each other.

Sadly, that wasn't to last and, as I was about to turn 8 years old, school became a place that I really didn't want to be and I had experiences that coloured my life in a darker shade than I wanted for the next 15 years. Life no longer felt safe, loving and nurturing outside of my home anymore and I was about to learn about the harsher side of human nature and the impacts it could have, short term and long term.

Learning Nuggets:

I have learned so much about the value of family and how our early years can shape us for the rest of our lives. My family experiences and our good memories never faded for me and no matter what happened in my life in later years, there was always a small part of me that knew I had a safe place there with my family, even if I didn't go to it when I really needed to and should have done so. Our families are often more interesting and complex than we believe when we are young and growing up. I found I understood and appreciated them more, the more I learned about them and researched my family history. We are the product of the generations before us to some extent and knowing where we come from is an important tool for self-awareness, I believe. Looking back years later, I am so grateful I had a feeling of being loved by my family as a child and I take that forward into my adult life now, understanding and appreciating the importance of family connections, stability and of having roots.

"Families are like branches on a tree. We grow in different directions, yet our roots remain as one" - Author unknown.

Anna Gray

CHAPTER 2 – SCHOOL'S OUT

I was about to turn eight years old and it felt like my school world turned on me. The people who had been my friends, suddenly and without apparent reason to me, at least, began to treat me differently. When I would arrive to school, they would distance themselves, whispering in groups and pointing as I sat alone eating my lunch. It happened quickly that I became more and more isolated from what I had felt was secure in my world.

I could find no justifiable reason for why I was being cast out by my peers. This was in the days before social media, so what was happening was contained within the four walls of the school and nobody else outside of it knew what was going on. When I turned up to school, most days would begin with the other children laughing at what I was wearing. I was never one of the 'cool kids' with the latest brands or trendy styles and looking back now I can honestly say what I wore was nothing out of the ordinary, it just wasn't 'cool'. The children would point and laugh, calling me a 'hippy' and a 'weirdo' or remarking on how I didn't look like them. Sometimes, it would extend to being pushed and kicked in the playground. There were trendy black shoes out in those days called 'Cheeseblockers', and when the thick black rim met my shins, the bruises were awful. It was always in secret, in corners unseen and without anyone there to defend me. I felt scared, intimidated and alone. Children would pull my hair, ripping little bits of it out. It was, and still is, a nightmare of curls and frizz if it's untamed and in the days before straighteners or styling products, I had no choice but to let it be wild and free. It was a constant source of embarrassment for me.

I was eating a lot of sweets, in secret, as a way of comforting myself so a few extra pounds around my waist led to further jokes about me being 'fat' and 'ugly'. I stopped being invited to my classmates birthday parties and sat with my head down while the invites were handed out to nearly everyone but me, the rejection cutting deeply like a knife. The boys in my class also joined in at times, when we had Valentine's day cards going around, not only did I never get one, but they would joke about how no boy would ever want to kiss me or hold my hand. Once or twice, a boy would make an offer to meet me during lunch and 'be my boyfriend', in the innocent way that kids became an item then in the 1980's in my school, by holding hands and pecking each other on the cheeks. I was very much in need of feeling wanted and accepted by that stage, so I would go at lunch to meet them, only to find a group of boys huddled together laughing that they had set me up again and I would walk off with tears streaming down my face. Notes would find their way around the room and to my desk, making fun of my face, my hair, my nose, my clothes...anything at all about me.

It was a desperately difficult feeling to have at such a young age, to feel so freakish. I would look at the other girls in the class with their pretty pink lunch boxes and perfect hair, colourful clothes and cute pencil cases with scented rubbers and I would feel completely out of place. I wondered that I might be absolutely pointless as a human being, worth nothing to anybody and just simply not good enough at anything. I became invisible to myself. When teams were picked for sports, I was always last. When children were picked to represent the school at events of any kind, it was never me. Whenever school trips occurred, I found I always got sick just before them, whether that was due to a fear of going in case I was bullied further or due to the stress my body was under, it meant I was always the one who was left out. I simply felt incredibly alone, unwanted, afraid to speak about it or ask for help and somehow unlovable.

I tried a few times to become part of the group again, I would do silly things to try and make my classmates laugh, in the hope that they might find me funny enough to want to be around. I turned up one day and went into the bathroom to spike my new short hair up and tried to make light of the bad cut. The entire class pointed and laughed and shouted 'Freak!!' as I sat down. Being laughed at, rather than laughed with, was not the outcome I had been going for. I stopped looking in the mirror and I stopped trying to fit in or to be included in things. I stopped hoping it would change and slowly accepted that I just didn't belong, that there was something about me that meant I just wasn't as good as everyone else and that the children bullying me must be right about me after all.

All I knew was that it hurt so much I could barely get up every day to attend classes. I had never experienced rejection before and it confused me, as well as deeply hurting me. I wondered what on earth had changed; why it was that I was no longer acceptable to them as a friend, as a person. For the first time in my young life I felt there was something inherently wrong with me, that somehow, I must be unlovable and strange.

Between the ages of nine and ten, it got worse; the names became more offensive, the insults more deeply personal, and the isolation even more evident. Every day there was taunting of one description or another, every day I sat in the silent agony of ridicule. Perhaps it was my sensitivity that made me such an easy target, perhaps it was that I was just too different from the crowd, either way, life became hellish. Being bullied and excluded was genuinely painful in a way that is difficult to portray in words. Without any social inclusion or positive reinforcement from my peers, I lost all sense of self-worth, self-esteem and confidence. I didn't reach out to tell anyone what was going on. It all happened out of the teacher's eyesight. I sincerely wish I had reached out but I just didn't know how to at that particular time. This was to come back to me again later in life.

Over time, I began to lose any sense of joy for life and everything about me changed. Once outgoing and bubbly, I barely spoke unless I had to. I couldn't look people in the eye and I found that I had no energy to do my schoolwork. I chose clothes that didn't suit me so as not to stand out and scraped my hair into ponytails with no effort involved. Once with long, curly fair hair that bounced into ringlets when washed, I saw no point in trying to look pretty or wearing my favourite things. I constantly compared myself to everyone else, forever finding reasons why I wasn't as pretty, as clever, as popular or as interesting as others might be. The more isolated I became, the more I grew to genuinely dislike everything about myself. I couldn't look in the mirror without finding extreme fault in what I saw looking back at me, so eventually I stopped looking. I couldn't bear the sound of own voice, so eventually I spoke as little as I could get away with.

My skin became very pale, transparent almost, as I wasn't sleeping properly and I didn't want to eat much good food. All this was noticed by my nearest and dearest of course, but I was determined to hide or explain away what was going on in school and inside me. I was taken for blood tests to check for vitamin deficiencies, as I looked so ill and was asking for time off school all the time. The baffled faces of my parents became a common sight and I denied there being anything untoward going on so often that it left them no choice but to believe it, or at least try to. I cried every night for a year, and I do mean every night, into my pillows so nobody would hear me externalise my hurt. The pain of waking up every day to face even more bullying made me so indescribably unhappy that I secretly wept constantly and went inside my shell so much that I felt I would never have any sort of real friendship again. It truly destroyed my life as I used to know it.

One night, after I turned eleven and would be leaving the school in a few months, I was lying in bed unable to sleep again. I had been reading as I always did to try and escape my own world and get into another more exciting and appealing one. The book was called 'Black Beauty' written in 1877 by Anna Sewell. She wrote it in the last few years of her life when she was house bound as an invalid. The story was written from the perspective of the horse named Black Beauty, beginning with his young and happy days as a colt in rural England, to his difficult later years as a taxi pulling horse in London. Throughout the story, he meets many hardships and recounts stories of unkindness and cruel treatment before his ultimate retirement to the country where he lives out the rest of his days in happiness and peace.

I had been horse riding for a few months by this stage and most of my books were horse-related. This one was the one I kept going back to again and again. Every chapter held a teaching related to the importance of the kind and fair treatment of horses. The story meant so much to me, as I felt I could relate to Black Beauty and his life because it held many similar traits to my own at that time.

I would lie in bed, reading his stories of hardship over and over again, sensing his utter devastation at the cruel twist of fate that made his middle years so full of pain for him. I cried tears every time I read it, as I recognised my own pain in his. Once young and full of life and joy, he found himself in an environment where he was unloved, unseen and treated unfairly. It was from then on that I felt a very unique connection to horses, an affinity that still remains today. Whenever I want to get away from everyday life and to feel my spirit soar, I will go horse-riding through a forest if I can, all the while tuning in to the power and strength and beauty of the horse, feeling those qualities enhancing the same in me. It's my little piece of heaven, to look into the eyes of a horse before mounting and taking off through the trees at the horse's own pace, both of us enjoying an escape from a dreary day of expectation and duty. One day I will achieve my dream goal of riding a horse on my own on a huge beach, not a person in sight and the sun on our backs. That feels like utter bliss and happiness to me.

Yes, there were moments where I did think that it would be better if I took my own life. I couldn't see how I had any sort of future whilst I was so desperately unhappy and alone. I believed the words I was hearing, that I was worthless, unattractive, unlikeable and too different from the crowd to ever have a normal life. The more I kept it all a secret, the more dying seemed like the only way out. I would sometimes lie in bed and try to imagine ways by which I could do it. I didn't want to be in pain anymore and it all seemed too far-gone to confide in anyone about. It felt like it would be too much of a shock to give to anybody to confess my emotional state and I saw no way to fix it all. I thought that, if

I could find a way to die that didn't involve too much pain, too much planning or too much activity on my part, that it would be a blessed relief to leave the earth. I believed that if I could just slip away somehow, in a way that wasn't too traumatic for me to do, or for the people who would find me afterwards to see, then that was the problem solved. I was barely 11 years old, but the world felt too awful to live in, I simply didn't want to be in it anymore. I had the thoughts and the feelings, but I never acted on them. I always somehow knew in my heart that I wouldn't, but the desire for the bullying and subsequent pain to end would often wash over me and take over to the point where I was immobilised with it, lying in bed and dreading the next day.

One such night at eleven years old, I was lying in bed feeling incredibly sad and staring into the dark. Slowly, a light began to form in the corner of the room and I rubbed my eyes, convinced I was so tired that I was seeing things. The light got bigger and brighter with blue hues around it and there was an immense sense of stillness in the room. I couldn't believe what I was seeing and I sat bolt upright in shock. The whole room was in darkness, with no streetlights or house lights, nothing to logically explain what was transpiring in my bedroom. I wasn't in the least bit afraid, in fact, once the initial shock wore off, an incredible feeling of joy washed through me and my entire body filled up with relief and calm and peace. I had no idea what it was that I was experiencing and I had never seen anything like it before. The light remained in my room for only a few minutes, but in those few minutes some deep healing occurred for me. I finally felt able to talk to my family about what had being going on at school and, in turn, they were able to step in and help it stop by coming in and talking to the teachers, making them aware of what was happening. In turn, the teachers were able to talk to the girls who had been bullying me and with their behaviour being exposed, it came to a stop.

I knew it broke my parents' hearts that I had been going through that bullying for the guts of three years and hadn't felt able to tell them. They were very upset and angry that it was happening and extremely concerned about my welfare. It was a huge relief when the bullying stopped; it certainly meant that every day was easier for me and that the worst of the feelings and thoughts came to an end. I still wasn't generally accepted as one of the crowd or included in much, but the direct taunting was reduced by a huge amount, which was a big step forward. A lot of damage had been done to my sense of self by the whole bullying experience by that stage and it has taken years to heal it. I'm still working on it at times, but I never again felt that I didn't want to live because of it.

I'd love to be able to say that from that point onwards I was able to talk about and share my pain to my parents, to friends, to anyone, but I wasn't. Hiding my pain became second nature and normal to me, I had internalised so much in my late primary school years that my voice simply wouldn't let me speak when I needed to. I held my words in my throat, pushing them down to the point of it physically hurting. I had recurring throat infections and episodes of losing my voice entirely during the time I was being bullied. When it came to talking about my feelings, it just simply wouldn't come out. It was normal for me to hide what I thought about anything, to keep my opinions to myself and to just agree with the majority. I became a 'people pleaser', not wanting to attract any disapproval or negative feedback. I had very weak boundaries, not knowing when or how to say no, which would show in later years.

I often thought about what it was, that beautiful light that appeared in my room. I came up with many ideas and explanations in those early years. Truth be told, I always believed it was some kind of Angel, some kind of visitation, simply because it felt so loving and that healing occurred because of the experience. That set the tone for moments of crisis in my life. It has often happened at a crunch point that I've felt someone or something step in just when I needed it most. It was the beginning of my relationship with what I will describe as the 'other' world, the first time I truly saw and believed that there was more than what we can see with our human eyes. I never told anyone about the light in my room that night, it felt too special and personal to me at that time to risk it being dismissed or mocked.

It took me quite a number of years and numerous situations that highlighted my lack of self-worth to realise how deeply being bullied had scarred me. I was under the impression back then that once it stopped, I would forget it ever happened and be largely unaffected. That was definitely not the case. It was only when I began to formally study counselling to practitioner level and a range of other therapies that I was able to see clearly how profoundly it had eroded my sense of self-esteem, my self-love and my core identity. I was able to see how choices I had made throughout my life would have been made differently if I had had a healthy sense of self-worth. I realised I had been stumbling through life from one harmful situation to another, drinking too much as a teenager and running from relationship to relationship, trying to repair the damage that was done in my early years, and only succeeding in reinforcing it. I looked for love in all the wrong places and never in the right ones. I was afraid to have opinions of my own, or to stand up to someone who was in authority.

I'm finding it hard now as I'm writing and recalling this, to not implore my younger self to get help sooner, to tell everyone what was happening for me, to not sit in silence with it all. I can still hear and feel the wounded young and vulnerable child inside coming through in my words, despite my years of healing and professional training, it still really hurts to remember and I know some of what I am writing sounds as if I am that hurt child again because I am reliving it so vividly through this chapter. I didn't have it in me to be cruel to anyone and I was so innocent and naïve. In the fifteen years that followed, I layered trauma upon trauma, totally unaware of the pain that motivated me from an unseen place within me. I often wished I could go back and put my arms around my younger self and steer myself away from some of the choices I made that led me down some very difficult and challenging paths, of which I'll share in coming chapters.

There wasn't a large amount of information available in Belfast in the 1980's and early 1990's about the long-term impacts of bullying and later in life. Nobody in my life, home or school, had the information to know the possible emotional, social and psychological ramifications that could come after it stopped. Mental health was still a taboo subject when I was young, it was a lot more difficult and complex to admit that something was wrong and you didn't feel happy and healthy. In my early 20's, when I came to study counselling, psychotherapy and gestalt therapy I wanted to find out more as I felt that my life had been affected by it on a deep level and in ways I hadn't understood when I was younger.

My professional studies, my own counselling sessions that I attended and some of the Spiritual Practises that I later came to partake in have all shown me that being bullied has had far reaching consequences for me throughout my life. I was, over time, able to heal a lot of the impact on me, but not without some years of unrecognised pain and negative actions that sprung from it. Indeed, an article that stood out for me recently was: 'Impact of Bullying in Childhood On Adult Health, Wealth, Crime and Social Outcomes" where the authors found through their research that: *"A large cohort of children was assessed for bullying involvement in childhood and then followed up in young adulthood in an assessment of health, risky or illegal behavior, wealth, and social relationships. Victims of childhood bullying, including those that bullied others (bully-victims), were at increased risk of poor health, wealth, and social-relationship outcomes in adulthood even after we controlled for family hardship and childhood psychiatric disorders. Being bullied is not a harmless rite of passage but throws a long shadow over affected people's lives."*

In my situation, there was no clear explanation as to why I was singled out by the bullies; there was no event or occurrence that sparked it off. I'm still unable to fully explain why it was me it happened to. The way I see it now is that it helped to form my frame of reference for years and the path of my life to some degree. Although it's impossible to accurately measure to what extent, there is no denying that it shaped how I felt about myself and the world around me.

I count myself lucky that I had opportunities in later life to work through all those impacts and to heal from them, as not everyone who has been bullied has that same chance and if my experiences and learning can help anyone else then I'm grateful for that. I don't look back in anger and I am very glad to see so much awareness and informed research around bullying available online and through organisations in recent years, undoubtedly it will help in some ways to de-stigmatise the whole issue and hopefully make it easier for children to come forward if it happens to them. I do wish the information had been as accessible when I was growing up, as it would certainly have made a difference to my life. I take heart in knowing that my experience, and how I healed the impact of it, can now help someone else who is experiencing it.

Learning Nuggets:

Going through bullying at any age is a devastating experience, debilitating and damaging to self-worth, self-esteem and our sense of personal power. Disclosing what is happening, reaching out for support and asking for help is not always easy, but it's the first step in stopping it happening and getting assistance. As a child and as an adult, positive reinforcement and emotional wellbeing are essential to our mental health throughout our lives, whatever our age. If I could take anything from that time of my life, it would be the importance of treating each other as equals, with respect, kindness and sensitivity - coupled with a knowing that we aren't a failure somehow if we are going through a hard time. I believe we all deserve a happy childhood, one where we are loved, encouraged and accepted for who we are. In childhood, we are building the foundation upon which we will live the rest of our lives, so trying to make it a positive and strengthening time goes a long way to becoming a happy and healthy adult.

The short and long-term impacts of bullying are very real and my experiences have certainly made me very aware of that. One negative or hurtful word or action can last for a lifetime, so I always try to remember what I learned through those years and apply it in my life now. I would encourage anyone who is experiencing bullying of any kind to speak up and to get help.

Letting it go to the point of feeling that life isn't worth living is heart breaking and there is help out there if only we ask. I'm serious about raising awareness of positive mental health in children and adults and I think the shame around admitting we are struggling with our mental health is getting less as more and more people come forward to talk about their own experiences in the media and through many mental health awareness events.

A quote to finish

"In the end, people will forget what you said, people will forget what you did, but people will never forget how you made them feel." - Maya Angelo

Anna Gray

CHAPTER 3 – FEATHER BOAS AND FREEDOM

I was fourteen years old in 1995 when I first went out to a bar in Belfast. I was supposed to be at a friend's house and we decided that we would try to get into a Gay bar in the centre of Belfast. We chose that bar because it didn't have bouncers or door security so, therefore, we thought we would be able to get in without our age being questioned. I went early at 8pm and dressed up as well as I could. I was there because I thought that it represented freedom and fun. I didn't know then that I was running from myself and finding some form of unhealthy escapism. My friend and I danced for hours, wide-eyed and amazed we had made it into a bar at our age.

I found it exciting, being in an adult's world. I didn't feel like a child at fourteen, but in reality, I was exactly that. I had saved up my pocket money, as infantile as that sounds, and I had saved enough to buy three Sambuca shots. I lined them up on the bar and the barman set them on fire, as was the custom. I drank them all in one go and the quick rush and blankness in my thoughts was immediately addictive to me. Suddenly, the world seemed bright, happy, fun and not harsh or hurtful. I made friends quickly; I had to as the friend who came with me the first night was moving away. The new people I met were all a lot older than me, I was the youngest in the bar by far and I was excited as I planned many more nights out. I would go early, drink and dance for a few hours and be home by 11pm. That happened about two dozen times, over a period of about six months. I always lied about where I was and had cover stories to back me up. It was a different world than what I was used to.

Anybody could express themselves through their dress, make up and dance however they liked to. Getting to know this small part of my society, where men dressed as women, where make-up and glitter and unusual dress were celebrated and where you could be anything you wanted to be, felt as if I was out of a constricted and boring life and into an exotic and free one. I had see-through dresses, PVC platform shoes, pink fur boas and glitter hairspray, and it felt great. I would leave my parents' house in jeans and jumpers, with a bag full of my stuff to change into. There were no mobile phones around for people my age in Belfast in the 1990's, so it was easy to lie and not be found out. Not straight away anyhow. It became a regular occurrence and soon I was drinking every weekend. I began to crave the buzz I got from drinking. I felt it was the only escape I had from a life that felt difficult to live in. I didn't realise it at the time, but I was living my life as if I was still being bullied even though this was no longer the case. I was still hearing the voices and criticism of my bullies ringing in my ears, but by that stage, their voices had become my own and I had adopted their criticisms as truth.

The initial excitement and buzz began to wear off as I turned fifteen, I noticed that when I drank, I wouldn't be energetic and happy anymore, I would begin to feel low, afraid and alone. Drinking stopped helping me to escape my own internal critic and instead began feeding it. When I drank alcohol, it opened up something inside me, a massive hole of emptiness, fear, loneliness and depression. A gaping chasm of utter hopelessness. Those dark and terrifying emotions would start in my stomach like a small ball and slowly grow, overwhelming me as they filled and took over my whole being. I would often be left incapable of functioning when that dark place opened up and I'd curl up in a ball in the foetal position and try to catch my breath as a deep sense of despair threatened to swallow me. For the few days that followed when I was drinking, my thoughts always turned to critical ones of myself and I often felt as if there was no hope for me.

I felt as if there was a huge black cloud over me at all times, that it was just waiting to envelope me into a darkness that spiralled me downwards into a place where I was unable to move, barely able to breathe and just to pray quietly through my tears that it would pass. Weekends were spent at the ages of 14 and 15 trying to get away with drinking without being caught and much to my sadness now, I was a brilliant liar. I managed to do it most of the time. I felt like I needed it, I craved it; it blocked everything out for a few hours until that awful thud would hit my gut and I knew the tidal wave of darkness was coming again. When I was caught by my parents going to bars, I would go to a park instead. They had overheard me talking to a friend on the house phone organising a night out in the bar, so I had to stop that and find other places to drink. When the police came and took my name and address for public drinking in the park, I went to a friend's house instead at the weekends for about three months. I always found a way. What felt like fun for a few hours, always became an episode of self-loathing for a few weeks following and so the cycle would continue.

My young body was suffering badly from it, I had no energy, I looked ill, I couldn't concentrate on school work, my face was puffy and pale and I slept too much. I wasn't drinking every day, but every weekend was still too much, bottles upon bottles of cider, rose wine and Sambuca shots took their toll. There were a few things that happened next in my life that are very hard and complex to write about, but they are important because they added to my unhappiness at a time when I was really quite impressionable and vulnerable. The experiences did scare me into not drinking so much but they further impounded my mistrust in people and in the world in different ways, only serving to deepen the wounds I carried around inside with me everyday.

The first was when I was sixteen and had lied again about staying over in a friend's house and had gone to a bar. I had been out for an hour or so and had only had one drink. I was actually quite buoyant and just really enjoying the music, I wasn't drunk and it was still early. There was 90's music playing and the bar was busy and full of laughter. A man I didn't know offered me a drink. I didn't feel I had any reason to suspect him as he seemed polite, well dressed and non-threatening. In my naivety I accepted the drink and took a few sips while dancing around the floor to Natalie Imbruglia's "Torn'.

The next thing I remember is thinking that the floor was coming towards my head and that I had a split second of time to stop it, which wasn't possible to do as I had no control over my body whatsoever. Then blackness. Nothing. I had a vague recollection of hearing an ambulance siren in the distance and I can remember wondering who the ambulance was for and hoping they were alright.

I woke up screaming and crying hysterically at the top of my voice, bright lights were in my eyes and a blurred figure standing over me. I can only describe the crying as something similar to what a wounded animal might do, loud and howling and uninhibited. Someone was gently holding me down, as I seemed to be flinging myself around a bed. When my eyes cleared I could see the blurred figure was my Dad and I realised the voices were nurses. It hit me that I must be in a hospital. I looked up at my Dad and I'd never seen him look so worried, so upset, so in shock.

I looked down at my clothes and they were all ripped, I had the beginnings of bruises up and down my legs and I had no idea what time or day it was. My ribs hurt and I had vomit in my hair. A deep sense of panic took over me and I just cried and cried and held my Dad's hands. A huge well of pain swept over me as if my heart was breaking and a bus had hit my body. Dad told me it was 4am and that an ambulance had brought me in and that I had collapsed in the bar. Nobody knew who called the ambulance and when I asked I was told it was a 'passer-by'.

The nurses made the assumption that I had drank too much. They gave me a long lecture about underage drinking and the staff raised their eyebrows when I tried to explain the next day that I'd only had one drink, and that I had felt fine and hadn't been drunk. I had no idea why my clothes were ripped, why I had bruises, why I had no memory of anything and why I had woken in such a soul-deep panic and screaming out.

It didn't occur to me at that time that someone might have put drugs in my drink. I don't think it occurred to anyone then, it was still relatively unheard of in Belfast. I was very confused at how I had ended up there, with only one drink and a few sips of a second. It wasn't until months later that I began to question if I had been drugged. It made sense, the loss of memory and the quick blackout tied in with the symptoms of being spiked with date-rape drugs. I still don't know exactly what happened to me that night, how I was bruised and sore around my body. I tried to remember something but it's all just a total blank, even now.

I spent the next few weeks apologising to my two very distressed, concerned and upset parents who did their best to ask me what was wrong, why I had lied, why I had been out, why I seemed so distant to them and what could they do to help. I couldn't fully open up, I couldn't put into words how I truly felt. Partly, because I didn't want to upset them anymore than I already had and partly because I simply didn't know how to explain it all. I wrapped myself up in cotton wool for the weeks following that, feeling violated, terrified, vulnerable and very alone. I had a huge amount of guilt around my behaviour and its consequences, I felt ashamed of myself and how my recklessness had put me in a position where I was unable to tell if anything more had happened to me while I was unconscious.

My biggest fear was that someone had raped me and I couldn't prove it. Although I thought I would know if someone had, that I would feel it, I had no way of knowing months after the event and I struggled with the sense of violation. I felt dirty, tainted, deeply hurt and incredibly angry. I felt something had been taken from me that I would never get back, whether I was raped or not, that loss of control over my own body and my choices left me with a strong awareness of my own vulnerability and fragility. I was only sixteen and still felt like a child inside. At times, the realisation of what I had been exposed to horrified me and made me feel very small.

I felt helpless, I believed there was nothing I could do to find out, that I couldn't go to the Police as I had no idea who the man was and any drug would have left my system hours or days after that night. So I did nothing, and the bitter unfairness I felt ate away at me daily. I built a wall around myself for protection, lashing out verbally at any innocent boy or man who tried to speak to me. I had lost trust in the opposite sex and was developing a serious anger towards them. I resigned myself to the idea that I would never know the truth, not fully anyway. I coped by pushing the feelings and memories of the aftermath as far down as I could, not wanting to think, let alone talk, about it. It was only years later, age twenty-five, when I was studying for my counselling qualifications that I felt able to re-visit the experience and do some research on date-rape drugs and their effects to try to confirm to myself that my suspicions were well-founded.

I found some information through the NHS Website (www.nhs.uk) detailing the different types of date rape drugs and their effects. It gave some examples of the drugs, namely Ketamine, GHB, GBL and tranquillisers. The signs to look for to tell if you have been drugged were listed as loss of consciousness, vomiting, confusion, hysteria, memory loss and loss of balance to name a few. It certainly mirrored my experience.

At the time I was studying, I was lucky enough to be able to sit down and have a chat with a lady who worked for the Rape Crisis Centre and she spoke at length and confidentially about her experience of working with Women and Men who had been drugged, some who suspected they had been raped and some who knew it for certain. She told me how it was quite common to withdraw emotionally after such an event, to feel anger, hurt, mistrust and violation. Whilst not everyone may respond that way, I recognised every sign that she spoke of and, for me; it was further confirmation that I had been drugged. I later confirmed these findings with my GP, who agreed that she believed I had been drugged but confirmed there was no way to prove it at that late stage.

I wish with all my heart that I had asked for help at that point, I wish I had felt able to be honest about how I was, to share my feelings, my fear, my guilt, my despair. I believe now that I if I had, it may have prevented things getting worse over the next few years. That's one of reasons I wanted to study Counselling, I felt very strongly that having a safe place to go to open up was something that I wanted to be able to provide for people.

When I turned seventeen, I went to a concert with a friend, we went to see a band we both liked and thought we would be able to find a taxi home no problem as it ended around 11pm. I was still recovering from the ordeal in the hospital and it was the first time I had ventured out in the evening since it happened. At 11pm, we stood in the street trying to get a taxi and there were a few hundred people with the same idea. There were no mobiles then for us teenagers and all too many phone boxes in Belfast were either burnt out or covered in food and vomit from passers by.

We waited and we waited, it was creeping up on Midnight and I was beginning to panic about being so late with no way of ringing home. My parents had been so strict with me since I'd been in hospital and it had taken a lot of convincing for me to be able to cross the front door to see the band, even though it was somewhere that had no alcohol. By just gone Midnight, we decided to walk home; it would only take us 20 minutes or so. Walking the streets of Belfast at night can be scary at the best of times but this night felt even worse, there were large crowds of people and a lot of them were drunk. As we walked up the main road, I saw a group of men and women walking towards us and my intuition told me that something wasn't right from the start. As they neared us, they began to run at us and two men and two women began to chase me. I ran as fast as I could in the opposite direction, right into the path of a car who slammed on the breaks and just stopped as I sprawled onto the bonnet with nothing more than a bump to my leg. The car sped off, maybe afraid of being reported to the Police or of some kind of driving charge. As I turned around the men and women who were chasing me grabbed me and threw me to the ground, what exactly happened next is a bit of a blur but I know there were kicks to my ribs and legs. I lay on the ground, in the rain, in total shock trying to protect myself. I didn't know them and they didn't know me. It was a random late night attack from a group of people who were clearly drunk and out looking for a fight.

I heard a van pull up beside me and a man jumped out with an Iron bar, he waved it around at my attackers and they ran away. That man lifted me up and put me in his van beside a woman who was there too. I had no idea who they were and I still don't but my first thought was that they were taking me somewhere to hurt me even more. I sat beside them shaking and hyperventilating with fear. I'd lost my shoes and my coat was ripped but I'd managed to hold onto my bag. They asked me where I lived and as was quite normal in Belfast for the time, I was afraid to tell them in case of religious and sectarian connotations.

They gave me tissues and they told me that they had been looking around the area that night as they had heard a group of people was carrying out attacks. They said I was the third person they had rescued that night. I've never been so relieved to feel safe in my life. I didn't want to tell them my name and I asked them to drop me to a street that was a few away from where I actually lived. I walked the rest of the way home and let myself in my front door and called out to my parents that I was home and sorry I was late as there were no taxis. I crawled into bed and hid until the morning when they went out and I never told them about it. I just showered the next morning, cleaned up the cuts on my legs and threw my clothes out.

As an adult and a mother now, to imagine that my daughter would go through that and keep it a secret is horrifying. Why didn't I say something? The only explanation I have is that I didn't want to cause any more pain and stress to my family. I had put them through enough in recent years and the thought of causing more broke my heart. So, as was common for me, I internalised the experience, the pain and the trauma that it caused. I didn't utter a word to anyone about it and it could have almost been a dream if there wasn't an article in the paper a few days later about a spate of attacks that had happened that weekend in that area. I hid the paper, of course.

Needless to say, both those events deeply hurt me in different ways. They shocked me enough to stop me drinking in the way that I had been, I felt too scarred by what had happened to put myself in any vulnerable positions in Belfast at night for quite some time. I would love to say that suddenly I was transformed and I began to heal my problems at this point, but I wasn't and I didn't. My inability to share my pain was ever present and my tendency to self-destruct was strong. It just changed form when one way was getting close to being noticed or when I was caught out. I stopped going out at nights and felt a lot of fear at small things that would normally not cause anyone to be afraid. If someone looked at me sideways in the street I would jump. I avoided crowds of people at all costs and I didn't feel safe walking alone anywhere. I felt trapped in my own secret experiences and it had to come out somewhere.

That's when I began to hurt my body myself, in a few different ways. When the memories of what had happened to me came flooding back, instead of speaking, or telling someone, I would cut myself. It was never deep enough to scar and it wasn't very often, but when I would lift a knife and cut my leg lightly, it released something from me. Just a little bit of physical pain took it away from my heart and the self-critical thoughts out of my head, it was a release, a little bit of control, an outlet, a physical distraction from an internal hell.

The first time I brought a knife to my room to cut myself, I was terrified. I sat on the floor for an hour, just staring at it and feeling too afraid to use it. I looked at the blade and ran it over my left leg for a few minutes, feeling a mixture of fear and guilt. I scoured my thigh, just enough to leave a shallow cut that didn't bleed enough to need tissues, but deep enough to feel physical pain. I hid the knife under my bed jumped into bed, terrified at being found out but also drawn towards doing it again as it felt like such a release and a high. I would go on to cut myself once a week or so for a few months when I was seventeen.

I didn't know it then, but I was beginning to Self-Harm. Self-Harm is defined as 'Deliberate injury to one's self, typically as a way of dealing with very difficult feelings, painful memories or overwhelming experiences' (Mind For Better Mental Health – www.mind.org.uk).

It started with the cutting, but to be totally honest, the fear of cutting too deeply and getting found out was stronger than the sense of release and relief I got from it. It lasted those few months when I was seventeen until I stopped with the knife and would do other things instead. I would alternate between hitting myself in the stomach repeatedly while lying in bed to pinching my skin until it bruised to pulling out my hairs, one by one, compulsively, until I had small bald patches I had to cover by putting my hair up in pony tails. I began to feel like I needed a little physical pain to take away from the emotional pain I was experiencing.

Trichotillimania is known as a hair pulling disorder, it's an impulsive control disorder characterised by a long-term urge that results in the pulling out of one's hair. It involves stress and anxiety, but researchers believe it's a complex combination of factors that drive an individual to hair pull. Technically not a form of 'Self-Harm' it is referred to as a Body-Focussed Repetitive Behaviour (BFRB) that can be caused by life trauma and is intended to be self-soothing to calm ones nervous system (According to The TLC Foundation for Body-Focused Repetitive Behaviours).

When I felt anxious or stressed, I would start to pull out the hair on my head and collect little piles of it until the feelings of inadequacy or self-criticism went away. I found it gave me some relief from feeling anxiety as it distracted me and moved my thoughts onto something else. I do believe that for me, I disliked how I looked and there was something inside me that wanted to prove to myself that I really was unattractive, and having bald patches destroyed my looks all the more. However, I also did it when I was bored, deep in thought or when I was tired. I often didn't realise I was doing it until I had a pile of hairs in my hand and other times I made a deliberate decision to sit down and do it. I had two or three bald patches on my head that people began to notice, I rarely went to the hairdressers and when I did, I explained the bald bits as damage from straighteners. I was mortified but I found it very difficult to stop, sometimes I would do it so much that my arm would really hurt from lifting it to pull the hair repetitively.

I never went to the doctor about any of these ways I was hurting myself, I simply couldn't find whatever it was I needed inside of me to let it all come to light and to admit I needed help. I didn't even know there was a medical name or condition relating to hair pulling until I began my studies and by that time I had stopped. Without knowing that it was an actual treatable condition, I didn't know how to help myself to stop. The urge to pull my hair would subside when I was feeling positive, when I was more active in my day-to-day life and when I was exercising. The urge to pull my hair was on and off for maybe two or three years and did gradually reduce by itself. I didn't consciously stop doing it, the compulsion to do it just seemed to naturally subside with time and once I saw the bald patches growing back I knew I didn't want to put my body through that again. Sometimes, even now, I will notice that I'm reaching up and touching my hair if I feel anxious or worried about something, but I catch it straight away and I'm able to deal with stress differently now.

I wondered about my motivation to drink and escape life. I felt confused as to why the drive to get away from myself was so strong. I did link part of what I felt to being bullied in primary school and the impact of that on my self-worth and self-love. Going to Grammar school at eleven had been a very welcome change for me and although I wasn't one of the 'In-Crowd' between eleven and fourteen, I wasn't bullied. I did enter early teenage years with a sense of isolation from my peers and of not fitting in, so that, coupled with the emotional remnants of the childhood bullying didn't set me up well for a balanced and happy teenage experience. I believe now that because I didn't open up and I internalised my feelings, that it all built up and up into a huge ball and the bigger it got, the harder I felt it would be to talk about.

Later in life, I did entertain the concept of 'Inherited Family Trauma' as a small contributor towards my state of mind. In recent years, there has been more research done on the concept that trauma is passed down through generations in our DNA. This is called 'Inherited Family Trauma' and works on the premise that traumas experienced by previous generations can be passed down to us biologically in our DNA. This can mean that we are walking around imprinted in a way with anxieties, depression, phobia's and fears that we don't understand and see no reason for in our own experiences.

The book I read on this subject a few years ago is called 'It Didn't Start With You' by Mark Wolynn. Mark is a leading expert in Inherited Family Trauma and the Director of The Family Constellation Institute in San Francisco. His articles have appeared in Elephant Journal and Psyche Central and when I read his book, it really resonated with me. Bert Hellinger of the Hellinger Institute, the founder of Family Constellation Therapy, trained him. The concepts of the book made a lot of sense to me and I wondered how many members of my family were unknowingly carrying the traumas of their predecessors and acting out their pain

COMING OUT OF THE DARK

and if any of those traumas were unknowingly impacting on me. Inherited family trauma is not about apportioning the blame of our problems onto previous generations, rather it's about becoming aware that their experiences can impact how we are built as people, our frames of references and how we see the world and respond to it. Becoming aware of that can then in turn help us to heal it for ourselves and maybe even stop the cycle from going onto younger generations to come.

In an Inherited Family Trauma session I attended once when I was thirty-five, I wanted to work on a recurring emotion that kept coming to me when I walked through Belfast City Centre. I would walk down a main street and out of nowhere, would feel panic and fear and a need to run away. It was recurrent, so I noticed it every time I went shopping there and it bothered me. During the session, the facilitator asked if anything had happened in that street during the times in Belfast when there were bombs in the 1970's and 1980's and I didn't know. I had to admit though that the feeling when I was in the street was of utter panic and a need to run away, so I thought I would ask my family about it. I spoke to my mum first and she was shocked to hear the street name and how I felt walking down it. She confirmed to me that when she was pregnant with me in 1980 that she had been walking down that street and there was a bomb scare and that she had to run away really quickly, feeling terrified for her and my life.

For me, that was confirmation that Inherited Family Trauma is real and that learning about it can help to unravel some difficult emotions and responses to life that seem to have no apparent explanation. I don't know if I'll ever know the extent, if any, that Inherited Family Trauma was a factor in my impulses to drink and escape, but it was certainly a really interesting subject to learn about and to understand more of.

Learning Nuggets:

Learning about Inherited Family Trauma changed my perception about the things that we suffer that we may not understand – I saw that not everything is down to experiences that we have had ourselves and that sometimes we carry things from the people related to us, even ones we may never have met. For me, that meant I was able to work on healing emotions and patterns in a way that I would not have been able to if I didn't know about it. That concept also made me very aware of how my experiences may impact on future generations, giving me a deeper understanding of others and myself. how my own trauma and that of my clients shows up and manifests.

Furthermore, learning how pain and trauma can manifest in self-destructive behaviours has been invaluable for me through my experiences of drinking, self-harm and trichotillomania. I have found that burying pain does not work and that it will inevitably show up and come out somewhere, somehow. For that reason, it reinforces my belief that talking and sharing our inner most feelings is imperative to living a healthy and balanced life.

I found an interesting quote on self-destructive behaviours that I think is worth considering;

"Before you pass judgement on one who is self-destructing it's important to remember they usually aren't trying to destroy themselves. They're trying to destroy something inside that doesn't belong." - JmStorm

Anna Gray

CHAPTER 4 - BREAKING THE CHAINS

This chapter details just some of my experiences of what is not commonly termed Intimate Partner Violence but may also still be referred to as domestic violence and is a difficult one to even commit to screen and then paper. I am writing about my own personal experience of emotional, physical and mental abuse in a relationship and this chapter is written solely from and about my own journey through this experience and how it felt for me. I'll delve into the difficult and dark places within me that the experience took me to and detail how I got help and transformed through it.

My intention in sharing all of this is simply to be of help to others who may have experienced something similar, are they right now or know someone who is or was there. Of all the chapters I'm writing, this one has to be the one that has weighed the heaviest on me. There are lots of reasons why I've found this part of my story difficult to tell.

Firstly, it was a very difficult time for me and one that is still painful to remember, even now years later. It's a lot more than that though. While it's important to me and to the story I'm telling that I'm open about this time of my life, I also feel like I want to protect the people who love me from the pain of reading it. I also needed to make sure that I am representing the whole experience in a way that feels true to me and there's a mixture of emotions and thoughts that are involved. There is a balance that I'm trying to strike here in regards to putting across how wrong it was, but how I have come, over time and with the right type of help for me, to not only survive it but to thrive after it.

It destroyed me and who I was at the time. I lost what little confidence I had in myself and all trust in men. I became a recluse, afraid of my own shadow and my own voice. I stopped recognising my own reflection and when I looked in the mirror, the person looking back at me had no life in her eyes, no hope for the future and a dreadful fear of life. There were moments where I was afraid for my sanity, moments I truly felt that I was losing my mind with the stress of going through that and of trying to keep it a secret. There were times I was so deeply immersed in it that I wondered if I deserved it, if it were my fault somehow. The fear of how far it would go and where it would end created turmoil for me in my life made me feel very ill at times. I barely slept during that time, my mind and emotions running wild. I felt so weakened by the abuse in every way, physically, mentally and emotionally that there were moments I wasn't sure I would ever survive it.

I'd like to share here in this chapter, a little of what I went through then, how it impacted on my mental and physical health and importantly, what helped me to overcome it.

I won't be sharing any details that will identify the man involved and there are a few reasons for that. The first reason being that my editor and publisher has intimated to me that to do so would leave me and my Publishing House in a position that we could be legally sued. That may seem to be protecting a perpetrator, however, even if I had the freedom to name him, I wouldn't. He was held accountable for his actions through the appropriate channels at the time and I'm satisfied that he has paid for what he did to me. It would serve no purpose to name him here in this book because what I'm sharing with you is *my* story, about *my* experiences, *my* feelings and how I survived it. This part of my story is about what helped me to survive a serious abuse of my vulnerability and how I transformed that pain into the sincere desire to help others. My intention in sharing this part of my life with you is that you might gain some inspiration or knowledge or hope from the ways that I came through it and what I learned from it.

Ok, now I've covered all that, I can take a deep breath in and begin…

So, there was a short period of time between the ages of sixteen and twenty-three that I was in a violent relationship. I loved the man, deeply. I entered the relationship with an innocence and hope that when I look back on it, breaks my heart because I didn't know what I would go through and if I could reach back in time and tell my younger self to run for the hills, I would. I'm also really aware now that I entered into the relationship with an already shattered self-esteem, a low self-worth and an inability to love myself enough to walk away. But I did love him, regardless of my state of being when I entered it.

It didn't begin with violence, quite the opposite in fact. We were drawn together with an intensity of emotion that knocked me for six. We were love-struck and high on emotion and couldn't stand to be apart for any length of time. I felt as if we had known each other for years, lifetimes even. He was romantic, expressive, and full of life and lots of fun to be around. I felt alive, loved, wanted, desired and, ironically, safe from the dangers of the world. Initially, his protectiveness seemed like a safe place for me. It didn't feel overbearing or like it was too much. It felt as if he was simply looking after me in a way that I couldn't do for myself. The guiding arm around my shoulders walking through town on a night out, the watchful eye on other men who made unwanted advances, the lifts in his car to places I couldn't get to myself.

Over time, the protectiveness increased and began to feel a little more like control. Around two months into the relationship things began to change and I could see the first signs of abuse starting to show. Suddenly, it was more than a watchful eye on other men, it was jealousy of them, that guiding arm turned into a vice-like grip that decided on my behalf to stay at home just in case other men might try to talk to me, those lifts in his car became a way of me being unable to go anywhere alone.

The first time he physically hit me was such a shock that I'm not quite sure I believed it were true. We had been shopping and he said that other men had been staring at me in a way he didn't like, that I must have been flirting or sending sexual signals to them. I wasn't, of course. With one blow to the side of my head, my remaining trust in men was gone. A huge range of emotions coursed through my body. Disbelief came first; utter shock as the truth sank in was next. I was surprised to find that those emotions were then followed by guilt. I felt guilt, as if somehow I had caused it and it were my fault. Then came the fear, I had no real idea he were capable of going that far or how far he might go again. Hurt followed, I felt all my dreams of the perfect relationship slip away in the swing of his arm. Sadness, or maybe a better word is grief. I grieved the image I'd had of him of someone who wanted to protect me from danger, not to be the one who created it. I grieved the innocence of our relationship and of our love; it was gone forever and could never be repaired. I knew I would never see him in the same light again and I was devastated that he wasn't the safe place I'd thought he was. I didn't feel anger right away and that shocked me, I wonder sometimes if I'd had more love for myself and a healthy sense of self-worth if I would have felt angry the first time he hit me, but I didn't and that didn't come until later.

Yet again in my life, I decided to keep it to myself and not to tell anyone. I would make a different decision if I had to go back and do it again. I hoped it was a one-off, a slip-up, and a bump in the road. In keeping it a secret, I didn't have to fully admit to myself or to others that it had happened. I was afraid of people's reactions, of any repercussions that may come if I told them. I wasn't fully ready to accept what it meant and to accept that the relationship was over instantly, I still had a small private hope that it could be fixed. Pushing it to the back of my mind, I carried on, 'being more careful not to give any reason for it to be repeated'. Please understand, I put that sentence in quotation marks because there is never something that anyone can do to give a 'reason' for being hit, but I was taking responsibility for it somehow, feeling to blame and feeling that I had to watch every little thing I said and did, incase it provoked a repeat performance. I was becoming afraid in so many ways. I was afraid to speak, to do my normal day-to-day activities, afraid to talk to friends and family incase they found out or spotted the signs. It was a horrible way to live. I didn't realise it at the time, but the feelings I had were the same as when I was bullied in primary school and I chose the same course of action – to keep it to myself. I can see now that another had replaced one form of bullying.

The second time he hit me was less of a shock, I had recognised the build up and the patterns from the first time. His paranoia that I would leave him for another man fuelled his violence on this occasion. This time, he hit harder but in places nobody would see, like the side of my head, my ribs, the tops of my legs. My fear of him increased and I began to be less and less myself. I dressed how he wanted me to, I changed my friends if he didn't like them, I spent all my free time with him and I did absolutely whatever he wanted me to do. I knew I should speak out, but I couldn't. I had become dependent upon him in lots of ways and I was afraid to be alone. My dependency on him grew with every passing week, I had no friends left as I had isolated myself, I had no money of my own as he gave me what he thought I needed, I had a very distorted idea that he needed me and loved me and that somehow his behaviour was partially my fault. I searched for ways that I could 'be better' and make sure his anger wasn't roused. I stopped looking at or speaking to any other man to the point of being afraid to lift my eyes off the ground when anywhere around. I hid what was going on very well and although my family suspected something was wrong, they didn't know the full extent of it. There were times they begged me to tell them what was happening and explained how they could see I had changed within myself, but I felt if I disclosed the truth then there was no way I could make the relationship work. My sister, in particular, sensed the situation was bad for me and would often try to talk to me about it but when she did I would push her away, afraid of her finding out the truth. My Mum and Dad really didn't want me to be involved with this man and if they had known what was really happening, I'm know they would have taken steps to remove me from the relationship. However, I hid it as so many people do when they are in abusive relationships, so I didn't give them the chance to step in and look after me. Now, years later, I can talk to them about it very openly. They can see how far I have come since then in my healing journey. I can see they are baffled and devastated that I didn't go to them for help at the time and that they are simply filled with gratitude and relief that I came out the other side of it able to help others in the same position.

Somewhere inside myself, I believed he was a good man at heart who was just troubled and in need of help himself. I still didn't feel anger and something inside me knew that if I ran from him before I had the strength to see it through, I'd be back to him as soon as the initial rush of escape had worn off and the fear kicked in. Inside I was dying, totally devastated that it was happening and completely terrified to leave. I felt trapped as if I was in an invisible prison, mostly of his making but partly of mine too as I still wasn't ready to give up on him and I still hoped 'he would change'. I took responsibility for trying to settle his paranoia, I was learning quickly how to appease his outbursts and I took the blame for things that only existed as problems in his head.

By the third time, I was broken. He locked me in a room with a knife to my throat after I'd arrived to see him later than I said I would be and he believed I was with another man, despite my proving I wasn't. I lost part of my tooth and any of my remaining dignity that day. Too broken to feel anger or to find any kind of fight within me, I looked unrecognisable, ill and drawn. I lay on the ground in total stillness for what felt like hours, staring wide-eyed at the dirty floor, frozen in terror and exhaustion and not able to find an ounce of strength. I believed on that day that there was nothing of 'me' left, that all of me had been beaten away by him, eroded into non-existence. I felt hopeless and resigned. I lay there and wondered what had happened to my life and how it had gotten there, broken and bruised on a dirty floor with no voice of my own to speak up.

There were more times he lashed out but it wasn't until the last time that something inside me woke up and roared like a raging lioness, if only for a moment. This time was sparked off because I had worn jeans that he decided were too tight and sexually provoking. I was lying on his bed and he was holding a metal dumb-bell to the side of head, about to smash it against me. I had split second awareness that if he did, I could quite possibly die from it or be left brain damaged at least. He had already kicked me around the bedroom and he was drunk, so I'm not sure he knew how far he would go himself at that point. I don't know where I found the strength from but I pushed him off me and I ran out of the house. I know for sure that being that close to severe damage and possible death was the turning point for me. Despite the fact that my self-esteem was at an all time low and I couldn't have thought any less of myself than I did during that period of time, my fight to live came back in that fleeting moment when I saw the dumb-bell about to come at my head. That day was the end of the relationship but it wasn't the end of the damage done by it. I had lots of work to do to reach that point.

Once I was away from him and the violence, I had time to take stock of it all and how it had impacted upon me. I needed time to examine it, to talk about it, to heal from it and to grow stronger. I needed to understand how I had ended up in that relationship and why I had stayed after the first time he hit me.

I made the decision to attend counselling sessions with Women's Aid, a charitable organisation that offered sessions for Women who were victims of violence within relationships, as well as other services.

The first day I walked into a counselling session I was terrified. I couldn't look the counsellor in the eye and I could barely open my mouth to speak to her. I had no idea where I would begin or how to explain what had happened to me. The room was so welcoming with a few lamps, scattered cushions and a discreetly placed box of tissues on the table. There was no rush, she said. It took me three weeks just to tell her the truth of why I'd come.

When I opened up to her and told her what had happened to me, it was so painful. Hearing the words out loud from my own mouth made it all real somehow, it wasn't my secret anymore and there came a huge fear with that. I was terrified of him finding out I had talked about it, I was scared that somehow I would be forced to talk to police or that I'd have to tell other people about it. Although I had left the relationship, I was still living under the shadow of it, it felt like I was still in it. I could still hear his voice in my head telling me to keep quiet, that nobody would believe me.

I shook like a leaf as I spoke, I couldn't look her in the eyes and stared at the floor as I spoke. I told her everything, every time he hit me, every word he said as he did it, every way he tried to control me and make me small. I knew my voice sounded weak and without any strength at all. That's how I felt as a person, weak, broken and without any strength. The counsellor waited until I had stopped talking and she looked me in the eyes and she said a single, simple statement that opened up the door and allowed my healing journey to begin. She said ...'I believe you.'

The instant relief that statement brought me was profound and I felt myself reel in shock that I had spoken the truth and that I was believed. I knew it was the first step but there was one more thing I needed to hear. As if she knew what I was thinking she gently added...'And it's not your fault.'

I broke down in that minute and sobbed and cried until my heart was sore and there was nothing left inside me. I felt as if a world of burden had been lifted off my body with those two statements she made and I knew I could begin to work through it all and the impacts of it and begin to heal from it. As the weeks went by and I continued to go to counselling, I discovered a huge list of ways that the relationship and the violence had affected me and was still alive in my life even though I was away from it. Once I knew I was in a safe environment where I was believed and held with respect and care, I felt I could explore it all in depth.

I'd like to recount the stages of the healing journey I went through during my time in counselling. It may be similar or completely different from other's stories that you may have heard or read about or maybe even experienced yourself. There is no formula for this and I can only share how it was for me, what helped me, what didn't help and the healing and growth I gained through it.

Over the coming weeks of my counselling I discovered that my healing and recovery went through various stages. The first thing I noticed was that once I was being heard and held in a safe place to talk about what had happened, I stopped normalising it. I believe that having another human being reflect the distortions I had about it back to me made me realise just how wrong it was. I had been living the secret life of an abused woman for a while and I had somehow convinced myself that it might be normal, that maybe it wasn't that bad after all. The more I spoke to the counsellor about the whole relationship, the more I was able to see that my own views and beliefs about his actions and myself had been conditioned and twisted. For want of a better phrase, the 'wrongness of it' began to sink in.

After that, I think I went into shock for a while. I hadn't realised how far gone I was into the darkness of feeling to blame and responsible for his violence towards me. I started to feel as if big chunks of a life I had built around me where falling away like heavy clothes that had weighed me down. I could see how I had excused it and tried to 'manage' it somehow.

I felt enormous fear at that point, a very real physical feeling that I was falling with no floor underneath me. So much so, that I actually had to lie down on the sofa in the counselling room and hold on to the sides of it to try and get some kind of footing or grounding. My worry was that I didn't know what was real anymore, I didn't know who or what I was without him and the relationship. If all I had believed about him and I was false and distorted, then what was there to believe and where did I go from here? I was alone for the first time since I met him, truly alone, without his shadow or influence. In a strange way, before he had started to be abusive, his protective nature at the beginning of the relationship had made me feel safe and that was all shattered now. He had become the danger. I was going to have to re-learn who I was and how to go forward alone, I was going to have to learn to feel safe in the world on my own.

Some weeks later into the process, I felt intense sadness and grief. I was devastated as the realisation of how toxic and unhealthy the relationship was began to sink in. I wondered how I hadn't seen it straight away and how I had let myself stay in it. I grieved the friends I had lost through it because I had isolated myself to keep it a secret. I grieved the opportunities to enjoy life that I had missed while I was immersed in the darkness of it. I grieved the strength I had before I knew him. I grieved the future I thought we might have had together if only he had 'changed'.

This was the hardest part of the process for me, the final acceptance of what the whole experience had been - a toxic and abusive relationship and not the 'Love' I had wanted to believe it was. I was learning about the short-term impacts of abuse through my counselling sessions and I related to most of them. I had low confidence, a feeling of being in a high state of stress and anxiety, low self-esteem, hopelessness, powerlessness, shame and guilt and rage.

It was only here at this point that I finally began to feel real anger. Once I realised just how much of my own self had been eroded and controlled and beaten down through no fault of my own, a sea of rage began to rise up from within me. The first wave of anger was venomous. I would wake up in the night screaming hatred and imagining ways to get revenge. I would play out conversations in my mind all day thinking of all the awful things I would say to him if I saw him. When I felt like that, I would go somewhere alone and scream as loud as I could over and over again until my throat was sore and the anger had released. I would punch pillows, go running, and play songs that related to my feelings and sing along at the top of my voice. I wrote pages upon pages of stuff that helped me to get through those painful days. I was always a big believer in writing my feelings down as a way of working through them, it helped me to read them back and to make sense of things.

Through my counselling journey, I could see how I had entered the relationship with low self-esteem, a need to be loved, a fear of the world and very few healthy boundaries. I hadn't really known who I was as a person and had already felt less than worthy of respect, care and genuine love. I think because of that, I was easily invaded and controlled. I knew I needed to learn how to love and care for myself and set clear boundaries of how I wanted to be treated. I needed to find out who I was and begin to transform that experience into something that would help me to grow and become the person I wanted to be. I wanted to heal from it; I didn't want it to define me. I wanted to be able to use the pain I went through to help others. I didn't want my view of men to be coloured by what had happened for the rest of my life, but that took a lot of time. For at least a few years after I ended that relationship, I both disliked and mistrusted men. I imagined every man to be the same as him; I was on guard most of the time with a hyper-vigilance and anxiety that ran through me. I was afraid that I would never have a successful relationship after what I had been through with him. It took time and a lot of beautiful male friends and role models to heal my mistrust and allow me to open up to a man again.

My journey was not a smooth straight line, once my counselling was over I often reverted to feeling bitter anger, guilt and hopelessness in the following few years. I was diagnosed with depression by my GP and given anti-depressants, which I took until I, was able to gradually decrease them and stop altogether under his advice. I learned that domestic abuse is not something I just 'got over'; it was a long and difficult road with many bumps and potholes.

There were long-term impacts that I suffered from too over the years and sometimes still do. Domestic abuse has long term impacts that are serious and perhaps not as commonly known as the short-term immediate ones. When I began to study counselling myself, I did a lot of research into this topic and found that survivors of domestic abuse are more susceptible to Stress, Arthritis caused by traumatic shock, digestive issues such as IBS, chronic pain and fatigue, a lowered immunity to illness, muscle tension, Post Traumatic Stress Disorder and mental health problems.

According to a study by the 'World Health Organisation' titled "WHO Multi-Country Study on Women's Health and Domestic Violence against Women': 'Mental problems, emotional distress and suicidal behaviour are common among women who have suffered partner violence.' Furthermore, according to an article entitled 'Health Consequences of intimate partner violence' by Jacquelyn C Campbell (The lancet 2002- Elsevier):

"Battered women also have significantly more than average gastrointestinal symptoms and diagnosed functional disorders associated with chronic stress such as IBS."

Some of the issues that affected me are that I have Arthritis in my neck, caused by repeated whiplash-like movements. That can flare up now and again if I don't look after myself properly and rest enough. Massage helps me as well as hot baths and good supportive pillows. I can still sometimes be very susceptible to anxiety, which can trigger the IBS and gastrointestinal issues I was diagnosed with. Relaxation exercises and meditations for deep breathing helps me to manage anxiety when it comes and that eases it. I had severe periods of chronic fatigue and pain in the years that followed that was diagnosed as Fibromyalgia after many tests to rule out anything else. I still have to be really careful how much I push myself to do or it flares up and I'm out of action for a while. I do my best to manage all of these things and in general they don't impact me very often anymore. I don't hold the domestic abuse totally responsible for these conditions, but I do believe that the emotional and physical trauma generated by it contributed to the development of those physical conditions.

For me, it was a long process of recovery that took years, not weeks or months. I found many sources of help and forms of healing that helped me along the way that I will talk about in further chapters. It took time, but slowly I began to build my world up again. My focus turned from talking about him and what had happened between us to speaking about myself and my future and new experiences that I wanted to have. I started to repair the friendships that I had neglected and found that there was a huge amount of support there available to me.

The most important part of the healing for me was knowing that I was believed, heard, valued, safe and respected. Without that environment in the counselling room I can't see how I could have begun to recover. The help I got from counselling and from friends and family afterwards was exactly what I needed to start walking down the road of healing in the aftermath of the abuse.

Over time, I was able to heal my relationship with men and learn to trust them again but that took time and work. I was eventually able to see the man behind the fist and to come to a place of understanding that he was deeply troubled and in a lot of pain himself. In some ways, I was able to forgive him eventually, although that's always a work in progress. The idea of forgiving him made me reel in disgust and contempt for a long time but I knew that if I was going to live a life free from anger and fear that I had to at least try. I knew I didn't need to see him ever again or tell him that I was willing to forgive, it was for my peace of mind and growth that I needed to do it. I knew that if I held onto the anger that it would define me and that I might never be able to live fully. I felt that I might never be able to be in the type of beautiful relationship I wanted to have if I held onto him in my heart as some kind of scary monster who ruined my life. I surrounded myself with a couple of men who I trusted in the years following the abuse, I spoke to them at length about my pain and I found that when they held a safe space for me to express my feelings I began to regain respect and love for men again.

Deep inside me I genuinely wanted my ex-partner to heal and let go of his pain too so that he could live a life free from the pain he felt in his own life that drove him to be abusive. I didn't want anyone else to suffer what I had at his hands and although I never wanted to be around him again, in my heart of hearts I hoped he was also able to transform his life and heal his own pain. I do support the idea of violent partners getting the right therapeutic help to prevent re-offending. I believe that it will help to stop the behaviour once it is accepted by them that it is harmful and they gain an understanding of why they behave that way. If an opportunity is provided for a violent partner to heal their own pain, hopefully the behaviour stops with them and is not continued with their current or future partners or their children. I don't mean they shouldn't be held accountable and have to face the legal consequences of their actions, but if therapy is a way to help stop abuse, then I'm for it.

I would say that being in an abusive relationship and coming out the other side of it better and stronger has been one of the biggest lessons and hardest challenges of my life so far. Nothing I have experienced up to now has brought me into a place as dark and scary as that time. On the other hand, with the right help and support I learned so much from it about myself and I transformed my life into living with love, trust, hope and positivity. I now work with women and men who are victims of abuse and I use my own experience coupled with my professional qualifications to help them come through it. I am proud of that and incredibly grateful to the people who helped me along the way.

I don't believe that the process of recovery for those of us trying to heal from abuse is black and white or linear in nature. I have experienced it like a river – sometimes it flows and sometimes it doesn't, there are often rocks that hurt your feet as you try to walk forwards and sometimes a pool of beautiful hot spring water to rest in with the sun on your face. There can be storms that make the water rough and deep and uncertain there are days when it's calm and it feels as if everything is blissful and perfectly healed. Some days are better than others, but I like to believe I am always moving forward, just like the water in the river.

Learning Nuggets:

In a nutshell, this experience has taught me the value of healthy relationships based on respect and love. The long term damage of abuse and violence is devastating and to inflict harm upon another human being leaves both parties with many consequences to face and heal over years. We all deserve safety and tender loving care within our relationships and anything less than that is simply not enough.

Seeking help and being heard and believed transformed my experiences for me from pain into growth and healing. I understood the value at that time of asking for help and how damaging situations can carry on when we don't talk about it and keep our troubles to ourselves. Having a counsellor just listen and believe me was undoubtedly one of the first times I realised the value of being heard and of expressing myself. I learned I couldn't do it on my own and that it was OK to ask for assistance and support. Years of not asking had led me to that point. No man, or woman, is an island.

"Whenever one person stands up and says – wait a minute, this is wrong – it helps other people do the same." - Gloria Steinem

CHAPTER 5 – BEHIND STAGE DOORS

*I*t was 2001 and I was twenty years old. I'd taken a year out of Belfast and moved to Scotland to stay with some friends.

While I felt hopeful about a new start away from the memories of home, I was apprehensive about coping on my own so far away. I wanted to change my world around and make something of a success of myself but I wasn't sure what that would look like or how I would achieve it. I still felt useless inside, as if nothing I tried worked out and that I was somehow incapable of being happy. On the surface, I was hoping that being somewhere new would help me to forget what life had been like in Belfast, but I now realise I really was quite lost inside. I was searching for something, looking outside of myself for answers, for something to fill that big hole in my heart and my lack of self-belief. I was running away from myself and what I felt inside, the emptiness and loneliness that was the undercurrent of my daily emotions.

I applied for three jobs when I arrived in Scotland, two office-based ones doing admin work and also some retail positions. I didn't get an interview for any of them and I began to worry that I wouldn't find work at all. A fortnight into my new life there, I found a local café within walking distance of the flat I had a room in. I got a job working there after striking up a conversation with the owner and telling him I had just moved into the area and needed work urgently. My job was to make food and serve customers and it took up a lot of my time at the start of my move. I had the responsibility of opening up in the mornings and preparing all the food to be cooked and I liked the feeling of being depended on and achieving something. I liked meeting customers and getting to know them but it soon became obvious that I wasn't earning enough to pay my rent and buy food, never mind enjoy a social life. I worked as much as I could, but it was minimum wage and the cost of living was high. Soon, every week became a struggle to make ends meet and I often only had one meal a day as money ran out quickly. Instead of asking for help, I allowed myself to become more and more stressed about my financial circumstances. Everyone around me seemed to be doing much better, able to pay rent, buy food and go out at weekends and I felt embarrassed and ashamed that I wasn't making my new life the success that I'd promised myself and my family I would.

I know at that point all my insecurities about myself came flooding back in and swamped me. I felt like I had failed before I'd even started and the shine was coming off my big chance of a new life. I interpreted my struggle to make ends meet as further confirmation that I was a failure at life and that I was somehow destined to be unhappy. It felt as though everyone else knew a secret password to making life work and nobody wanted to tell me what it was. It was at that point in my life that I learned quickly how detrimental to our mental health it is to struggle financially. From morning to night it was all I could think about and basic survival became a preoccupation of mine so much so that I couldn't enjoy anything on a day-to-day basis. I judged myself very harshly against others who seemed to be able to afford to live comfortably and I took my inability to do so as a huge indicator that I was a failure as a person. My stress about it took over my thoughts and everything felt so hard, from basic shopping to paying rent. I worried constantly and tried to think of any ways I could make more money. I couldn't physically work any more hours than I did already, so I figured there had to be some way of making more money in a shorter time frame.

About 4 months into my time in Scotland, I was walking down the street and feeling really down about myself and considering giving up and going back to Belfast. In my heart of hearts, I didn't want to do that, not yet at least. I didn't want to go home with my tail between my legs because I couldn't make the finances work. I was always looking around for new work but there wasn't much I had the qualifications to apply for that would increase my income enough. I had left my Degree after the first year because I really didn't like what I was studying. I had picked English as a degree simply because I had no idea what I wanted to do long term as a career and I was good at it in school. Being good at it wasn't enough for me to be able to commit to doing a three-year Degree through to the end though and I gave up on it. I had no real direction for myself, no real sense of purpose and I felt lost.

As I walked down the street I came across a collection of bars and I realised quickly that they were Lap dancing bars. They didn't and still don't exist in Northern Ireland so it was a rare sight for me and I was quite shocked by it. I stood outside one of them and stared at the door with a mixture of feelings. Initially, I felt embarrassed but also intrigued. I had seen films where Lap dancing bars were depicted as quite glamorous and wondered if it was the same in real life. I knew I wouldn't go in that day to have a look, but as I walked away the thought came to me that maybe I could do that job, as a way to make ends meet. I quickly pushed that thought away as it felt scandalous and risky to enter into that world.

As the days went by, I couldn't get the bar out of my mind and I felt strangely drawn towards it. I felt that it could be an answer to my money problems but the fear of what it would be like was strong. I asked a friend to go with me to visit it and to have a look inside. We got our glad rags on that night and took a taxi down to the bar and giggled nervously before we went inside. It really was dark and damp and was nothing like the ones I had seen in films. I'm not sure the whole bar was much bigger than my living room in the flat I was staying in. There was an extremely small stage in one corner, barely enough for one person to stand on. There was no pole and the whole place stank of beer and cigarettes.

My friend and I sat down at one of the small round tables and exchanged nervous looks. From a door behind the bar, a woman emerged and began to walk towards the mini-stage. She had bleached blond hair that was growing out to show grey roots. She looked around fifty years old. She was wearing white underwear that had turned grey with time and use and her knickers had cigarette burns in them. She was smoking as she got onto the stage and leaned against the wall. She didn't meet the eyes of anyone there in the bar and stared at the floor as the music began. With no pole, all she could do was move a little on the spot to the music while she dropped ash from her cigarette around her feet. She moved slowly with no rhythm or zest and I immediately felt awfully sorry for her. She looked bored, disengaged and accustomed to being ignored by the audience. Nobody looked her way, nobody gave her money and once the song was over, she quietly got off the stage and moved back behind the bar and disappeared through the door.

My friend and I stared at each other in shock and disbelief – was this really what it was all about? It was nothing like the films! We left and continued on down the street and found another Lap dancing bar that looked a lot more modern and vibrant. We pushed the doors open and it was a different world than where we had just been. The women were dressed in the newest clothes; there was a buzz about the place, a young crowd and a busy night. My heart started to pound as the manager came over to us and offered us a drink. We accepted and sat down, a little in awe of it all. When he brought our drinks over, we got chatting as he asked me where I was from and we talked about Ireland for a while. As he returned to serve drinks, I felt a strong impulse to ask him if he needed any new dancers and to try and get work. I didn't think too deeply in that moment about why I was asking, I just did it. It felt like a solution to me. He told me he did need someone and asked me to come along the following night to try it out. He asked if I had done it before and I said no, but that I had danced Salsa for a few years. I was mildly offended when he laughed and pointed out that it wasn't the same thing at all but I shrugged it off and started to plan what I would buy to wear for the next night. I didn't have much money, but I guessed I wouldn't need to buy many actual clothes, more like new underwear and a few other bits.

A thing I noticed the first night I worked in the Lap dancing bar was the strange shape of the building. It was narrow but seemed to stretch back forever. I hadn't paid much attention to that when I had visited the previous night. The bar was high, with around six empty bar stools lining it; it had been varnished so heavily that it looked like I might slip off it if I leant on it. There was red velvet everywhere, which seemed like a cliché and mildly amused me.

There were five other dancers there, all shapes and sizes. Three blonde and slim women with big smiles and small waists, who had no interest in talking to me, a brunette with dead eyes who looked like she would rather be anywhere but there and a red head who I instantly liked because she squeezed my hand as she walked past me and whispered words of encouragement in my ear. I had been told that I would need to do a few dances up on stage with the pole and that they would be fully dressed. In between those pole dances was the time that customers would buy a token from the bar for a private dance and approach me with it. I would then keep all the tokens and trade them in for money at the end of the night when the shift was over. The private dances were not fully dressed I was told, they were to end up naked. I had no idea how I would do that and was trying not to think about that part.

My heart was pounding, waiting for the moment when I would be called up on stage. The club was filling up with men from all round the world, sitting with a drink in their hands and looking with eager eyes at the dancers, me included. My boots were cheap and too big; I'd bought them last minute, just as the decision to become a dancer was last minute. The black dye they contained rubbed off on the skin around my knees and they made me stumble a little when I walked. My dress was a joke, if it could even be called a dress. Tiny and easily removable was the aim I suppose, but tiny and easily removable felt very vulnerable and exposing that night. It was black and transparent and it tied at the sides so I could easily remove it with a few tugs. I didn't bother with a bra, but I had these amazing butterfly shaped knickers that also tied at the sides like laces.

When my turn to dance came up, I heard my 'name' being announced - "Crystal". Oh, how to explain that moment!?...The fear, the exhilaration, the hint of excitement. The stage floor was sticky from spills of beer and the pole really was like the ones you see in the films. I took a deep breath and closed my eyes as I grabbed it and wondered what the hell I was supposed to do. It suddenly occurred to me that I had never done this before, I mean, yes I had danced, but not pole-dancing! I didn't know how to move, how to look, how to make it look like I knew what I was doing. I laughed to myself as the song started, I couldn't believe the irony. It was 'Perfect Gentleman' by Wyclef Jean. It is literally about a lap dancer and tells the story of how she got into dancing because she had no way of paying for her tuition and how hard she found it. I couldn't believe the words of the song and how much they related to me as I danced on the stage. The songs we danced to were picked randomly by a CD player so it was a coincidence that wasn't lost on me.

I didn't look at the men who were in the audience, I just allowed myself to get lost in that moment, there was a tremendous mixture of thoughts and emotions pouring through me. I was really aware of being watched and admired and, for a little while, I felt ...attractive, seductive, in control, untouchable. I hadn't felt like that for a long time and I allowed myself to revel in those feelings for five minutes. It felt free, as if somehow I was coming out of a cage and let loose to be wild and free.

Looking back now, I can see that I was seeking the approval and validation of the men there to feel good about myself as I had spent a lot of my life feeling so bad about how I looked, but I didn't have awareness of that at that time. It boosted my confidence temporarily in a false and shallow way. I didn't actually like or approve of myself at all at that time and gaining the attention of the men there simply acted as a cover for that.

Once it was over, the claps from the crowd had died down; I felt a tap on my shoulder. Behind me stood a man with a token in his hand for a private dance. This was the bit I was dreading the most. To the left of the stage was the private lap dancing room. A curtain of the favourite red velvet covered the entrance and inside was red bench-like seats for the customers to sit on while they were getting a dance.

He was heavily overweight, with a light blue shirt on that had sweat marks in the armpits. His hair was mousy at best and his face told tales of high blood pressure and a high-pressured office job. He didn't even speak to me, just pushed the token into my hand and stared at the floor. It was the fastest five minutes of my life and it all passed in a blur of his beady eyes and me trying to work out how to get to the naked stage gracefully without falling over. I didn't have the time or presence of mind to think too deeply about how I felt.

I did a total of fifteen private dances that night and I earned enough to pay my rent for a whole month in those few hours. Some of the men were rude and I felt like a piece of meat dancing for them, not even meeting my eyes or chatting before giving me their tokens. Some of the other men were genuinely nice guys, slightly embarrassed themselves to be there watching me dance and making an effort to have a conversation. I actually enjoyed a few of those dances, there were some laughs and fun involved too. It was an interesting mix of dynamics and attitudes towards me and I wondered if how they treated me was a true reflection of their opinion of every women in general, or if was it just their opinion towards a lap dancer. I could easily sense who saw me as a piece of meat because I was dancing for them and it didn't feel good. I was much more drawn to dance for the men who treated me respectfully as an equal and maybe even with a little awe.

Walking home that night I couldn't wait to get to sleep, it had all been a shock to my system and I was overwhelmed by the contradicting emotions and thoughts running through my body. There had been moments when it felt fantastic, moments when I had felt like the most attractive and powerful woman alive. I felt a power over the men to tantalise them and I had enjoyed moments of not feeling like a victim. I realised though, that feeling only surfaced when I was at a distance from the men, when they couldn't reach me and I couldn't see them close up. There was no intimacy in that distance. The private dances, they were mostly a different story altogether. I had felt ill a lot of the time, terrified, violated, disgusted. The closeness of the contact was too much, there was no hiding place for me - and they could see me, all of me – I could feel their different energies and some weren't pleasant to experience. I could feel that some of the men had an utter disregard for me as a woman, for the vulnerability of being naked, for the sacredness of a woman's body. I felt used, disrespected, violated, cheapened and like I had sold myself out to some of the men I danced for. I imagined that some of the men could see how little I thought of myself at that time of my life and were able to take advantage of it. I realised it was me and only me who put myself in that position. If I had a strong sense of self-love and respect for myself, I would not have exposed myself to being used as a sex object. I may have enjoyed trying out pole dancing in a different context, without selling it for money.

As it worked out, I got a call from the manager the next day asking if I wanted to come back, I said no without explaining my reasons why. I just couldn't continue, the emotions it raised where too difficult. I still needed money though and I needed something in addition to my cafe job. Once the money I earned that night lap dancing ran out, I panicked. I returned to selling my sexuality and I joined a phone company as a Sex-Chat operator.

There was no training apart from how to log in to their system and some legalities about what could or couldn't be said and what to report if someone disclosed they were partaking in illegal sexual acts. The first night I was taking phone calls I was shaking like a leaf with nerves. I was doing an all-nighter shift from 12am to 7am. That was the busiest time apparently so I could make more money for being on the phone longer. I only got paid by the minute of actually speaking on the phone; so the longer I could keep a customer on the line, the better for me financially.

It was cold in the flat, so I turned on the heating and made myself some cheese on toast with a cup of tea. I logged in to the phone system and waited for the first call, I felt sick with nerves. The first call was a man who just wanted a chat about his life, thank God. He said he was lonely and just wanted to chat to a woman. I took all sorts of calls that night, from men who wanted me to pretend to be in my seventies and dressed up in PVC, men who wanted to dominate or to be dominated themselves verbally, men who had vile fantasies of crude bathroom activities to men who thought the whole thing was rather funny and hung up quickly in shame. I was gob-smacked. I felt dirty, used and tainted. I know sometimes that people can be curious about if the phone operator actually enjoys the conversations themselves – I really didn't.

The final call I took that night was the most unusual experience. It was 6am and the phone beeped, I picked it up and a woman was on the other end. Somehow, her call had got directed to me in her quest for a phone-tarot reading. The company I worked for did both types of calls, so clearly some mistake had been made. She was in tears and I didn't get a chance to explain that I wasn't a tarot reader and that she had the wrong service.

She launched into depth about her relationship break-up, the fact she would be selling her house and losing her family unit and her devastation at being alone again at the age of 55. I just listened, I didn't know what else to do, it felt wrong to cut her off. She just wanted someone to hear her pain at 6am in the morning so she wasn't lying in bed alone and afraid. She stayed on the line for an hour until I was due to log off, we spent that time chatting and by the end of the call she said she didn't need a Tarot reading after all and that just talking to someone had really helped her.

Well, I learned something that night about the power of just listening to someone and how cathartic that can be for them. I was delighted that I had been able to ease her pain, my heart felt full of compassion and care for her. I felt I had helped her healing process somehow just by being there to listen to her. Those feelings felt so much better than being on the phone talking about sex when I didn't want to be. I felt a strong pull towards wanting to help others that way again, to want to hold space for healing and transformation. In my heart, I knew I needed to be in that space first, before I could help another. I wasn't ready to be someone's counsellor yet, I had too many of my own issues, but it was a spark in the darkness that gave me a little hope.

As the morning came, I sat on my sofa and picked up a book I'd bought earlier that week about angels. I scanned quickly through it, getting a feel for it. It was about how to connect with your own angel and ask them for help. Fat chance, I thought, there were no angels around me recently, and even they had deserted me. I was sure that even they would be ashamed of me and my lines of work in the last few weeks. I felt my throat close over, that all familiar lump rising up and blocking my tears. I had no idea how I had ended up in this position, alone in a different country and so broke that I was doing what felt like a milder form of prostitution.

I felt like a cliché – a woman with no self-love or personal power who felt she had no option but to turn to selling sexuality in order to survive. I never had actual sex for money, but lap dancing and phone sex only felt like one step away from that for me. I was scared I would end up down that road if I didn't get my life sorted out.

I went to bed and wondered why life seemed so hard. It felt like nobody could spot my silent cries for help – no person I knew at the time and certainly no 'angels'. I gave the phone work up after a few weeks, it began to disgust me and I dreaded every single call. I wanted to pull myself out of this rut. I decided to go back home, to Belfast, and try to start anew. I had no plan or job to return to, but it felt like a relief at that stage to go back and join normality again.

I had dual emotions and two different things going on for me during my time in Scotland. Part of me felt like a victim, pushed by circumstance and fear into selling sexuality so I could survive. The other part of me felt like I had a sudden power that I could yield over men by using my sexuality, for my own advantage. So, on the one hand, I felt like a victim of men and on the other hand I felt they were my victims. My brain began to work out ways to manipulate the men into buying more tokens to get dances from me. I imagined I could be extra seductive, extra flirtatious, extra explicit and that it would improve my income. I felt a power I hadn't experienced before, although I'm not sure 'power' is the right word. There was a balance of power between the men I danced for that we were working out between us silently. I often wondered how much of that happens in real life, outside of the velvet room, how much do we barter with our sexuality for gain, how much are we victims of an abuse of our sexuality? How often money is held over women by men as a tool of power used to coerce us into acting or doing what they want? And how often do we knowingly manipulate men for financial and material gain? I have been in both boats, sometimes simultaneously.

I know that not every woman who lap dances or works in phone sex feels that way or gets into that line of work for the money. Not every woman feels disempowered by it or somehow beholden to selling their sexuality to pay their bills. I know women who do it because they genuinely really love it and feel no disrespect through it at all. They feel strong and happy with their choices, it suits them and fits into their lives and it doesn't diminish how they feel about themselves or about men. I can only write about how it was for me, why I did it and how it made me feel. I have no judgement of lap dancing or phone sex as good or bad, right or wrong.

It just wasn't a healthy choice for me because my reasons for going down that path came from a place of fear panic and survival. I'm not afraid of being a sexual person any more, as I was for a period of time following living in Scotland. There were memories of the way I was looked at and spoken to in the bar and on the phone that made it feel dangerous to be with a man sexually and I felt really vulnerable. I feel like I have seen quite a lot of the darker aspects of sexuality through those experiences and I have long since been able to decide on who and what feels right and energetically clean and healthy for me.

There's been huge healing and learning for me that has come through those experiences and although it was really painful, it has been massively beneficial to me and to others who I have helped in my work to begin to heal some of the guilt, shame, fear and abuse that we can feel around sexuality.

Learning Nuggets:

These experiences have taught me about the importance of having and only accepting a healthy sexual energy in relationships - filled with respect, love, care, responsibility and self awareness.

Reflecting back on that whole period of time in Scotland, I learned some very useful lessons about the dynamics of the relationship between men and women, mostly about the balance of power and how it can be abused by both men and women alike. It wasn't an easy time at all, but I also learned a lot of how financial poverty can severely impact on a person's self-worth and sense of security and just how far past our own values and boundaries we can go out of a need for survival. My sense of self was greatly eroded by being in a violent relationship and being able to lap dance and stand naked in front of someone didn't feel like it took courage or confidence – it felt like there was nothing of me left to protect and that I was simply an object to be used however other people liked. Learning that I am a valuable and sacred woman worthy of respect and care was a huge lesson throughout this period of time in my life.

The biggest lesson I have gained from it all is that no matter what situation I find myself in now or in the future, I will never put myself in any role where I feel I have to de-value myself again to gain some sort of financial security. I know now in my life that I am worth being respected, treated as equal, and held in safety and sanctity. Even if I was penniless, I would never walk down that path of selling an aspect of myself again. I'm also really aware of treating men with the same respect and honouring them with no manipulation, mind games or abuse of any sort and I live by that. I'll end this chapter with a quote that I came across that inspired me;

"She knows in her bones that a healthy sexuality and its full expression are not in opposition to goodness, rather they are in sacred service to the Divine" -vcc

Anna Gray

CHAPTER 6 – THE MAGNIFICENT MASCULINE

*A*rriving back in Belfast was very difficult for me emotionally. I was only twenty-one and it was 2002; early into a new decade and I just wasn't filled with any hope that this new decade could be any better for me than the previous one. I carried a big suitcase heavy with guilt and shame about my lap dancing and phone sex days with me on my journey home. I was also terrified that somehow people at home would find out and I felt I had let myself down.

It was at this point that I reverted back to my teenage years for a while and I began to drink too much again. The difference this time was that because I was older, drinking was more accessible and socially accepted. I was also carrying a huge dislike for men, an anger for them if I'm really honest about it. I felt that I had sold myself and that men had bought me. I had very little self-respect left at this point and I wouldn't have known a healthy boundary if it hit me up the face. I was in pain and I didn't know how to deal with it. So, I did the only thing I did know how to do. I found escape mechanisms.

The anger and hurt I felt around men pumped through my body everyday like an electric current. There was an inclination in me to hurt them back, to use them as I had offered myself up to be used, to discard them as I had been discarded. So, I did exactly that. I dated every man I could find. I had an embarrassing amount of one-night stands and I turned myself into a woman who never got attached. I drank and I went to every bar I knew of and life became a constant party. I became very emotionally numb, losing all sense that there was anything unhealthy in the way I was living. My heart was closed with the highest of walls built up all around it. And this hurt me even more.

At the time every man was an object to me, I had no emotions and nobody meant anything to me. My world was about illusory self-protection and preservation. It was easy come, easy go, as far as I was concerned. I was very good at the seduction part, using my lap dancing past as a hook to draw a man in, being incredibly forward and sexual in how I spoke to them, playing games with their feelings and having absolutely no remorse for it. It felt as if I was getting pay back, that I was finally the one in control and that I would never allow myself to have an open and gentle heart again. I foolishly believed that behaving that way was me 'getting my power back' and being 'a strong independent woman'. I really couldn't have been more wrong. I was a hurt and angry little girl inside who was acting out her pain on the opposite sex instead of diving into the depths of my pain and healing it. I didn't know how to do that yet.

Life had been this way for around eight months when the shell began to crack. In the midst of the madness of that time I had managed to get a job that I was quite proud to have. I was selling insurance that nobody really needed and was so good at it that I got promoted to manage a team of around ten people. I often look back now and think to myself that I was so good at 'talking a good talk' and selling something I didn't believe in that my job mimicked my approach to life at that time. I could talk a good talk about myself, I could sell an idea of myself as strong and happy to people and most people were fooled and readily believed it. That deeply saddens me, firstly because nobody knew the real me – the hurt and damaged place I was acting out of was not the true person I was. Somewhere deep inside I was still kind, gentle, generous, loving and fun – but I fiercely protected that so that nobody could hurt me again. Secondly, no real bonds of friendship or love had stood a chance of blooming because I was acting a part. I regret the connections of real friendship I had potentially missed. Thirdly, I know there were men whom I hurt along the way through my lack of care and respect for them. Being treated badly by men myself did not make it right or justified for me to take it out on other men.

I was socialising so much that I was exhausted and unfit for work. I felt genuinely depressed as if years of painful experience were catching up on me and I couldn't keep the lid on it any more. I was run-down and I felt spent. My life felt at a breaking point and as if everything was falling apart. I took a month off work and went to my doctor to ask for a sickline, who conceded that I could be depressed but didn't want to issue medication straight away until I had rested for the month. I felt a mixture of relief at being heard and helped and ashamed at having a diagnosis, it felt like a dirty secret and a taboo subject. I took the time off work to regain my strength and to take stock of my life and to decide on the changes that I needed to make. I knew I had to pull away from all the socialising and the dating and begin to look after my mental and physical health. I found at this time I was turning back towards my family for support. My parents and siblings were becoming people who I felt I could open up to a little more. I was beginning to realise that I had been shutting them out for most of my life and it was almost as if I was a flower, trying to grow and blossom even though I had cut my own roots away and disconnected from them emotionally. I couldn't get into the soil to soak up their nutrients. My feeling of isolation from them was lessening and although I still didn't let them in completely, things were getting better between us.

It felt like a turning point for me, a big wake-up call so to speak. I began to accept that I couldn't contain that amount of pain and deal with it all on my own any more. I began to feel like I desperately needed some help outside of my own coping mechanisms. I started to feel like I was ready to understand myself and the things that had happened in my life and how they had impacted me. It was a very slow process, but I was starting to understand I needed to take responsibility for getting better and in order to do so; I would need to reach out and open up.

It was around that time that I attended a workshop ran by a man called Ger Lyons. I had heard about Ger through a friend and she recommended his work. She had told me about the type of work that Ger did, called Cellular Transformation. The concept of this healing was that we hold every memory, every trauma and difficult time we experience in the cells of our bodies. This can, in time, turn to illness, sickness, disease and creates patterns of behaviour and belief systems that can be unhealthy for us. As an example, imagine you experience growing up in a household where there is no money and you are always hungry and feeling like there just isn't enough of anything to go around. As a consequence of this, it's entirely possible that when you grow up and start to go out into the world on your own, that you carry this memory and belief even though you aren't in that exact situation any more, that you believe there is no money to be had and that you will always be poor.

As a result of this buried belief and pattern, you go into jobs that are low-paid; you get into debt and continually reaffirm your idea that you will have nothing. Now, all the while this is going on, you may be feeling frustrated, desperate to create the type of life and security and abundance that you didn't have as a child and you may be feeling totally in the dark as to why you can't achieve this. And so the cycle continues.

Cellular Healing works on uncovering that sub-conscious belief and working on healing it. Whatever your preferred terminology, it works on the belief that there is a Universal Force that has an intelligence much greater than our minds and that we can ask it for help to release these unhelpful and painful memories from our systems, therefore, leaving room and space to create new, positive ways of being. I like to describe it as a computer programme.

What that actually means is, we are programmed by our environment as soon as we are born. Like a computer, our parents input information, as do our siblings, friends and teachers. Before we know it, or have a chance to disagree with it, our entire outlook on the world (our frame of reference, if you like), has been programmed into us like we are computers, without our awareness. We run this programme over and over every day on automatic mostly, very rarely realising that we do have the power to change it and to re-programme ourselves in a way that we would prefer to operate, a way that brings us the life that we actually desire to have. More often than not, these beliefs are not ours at all, they are the ones formed out of the experiences that the previous generations have had and they pass them on to us. Whether we like it or not. Whether they suit the world as it is now or not. Whether they are the actual truth or not. Worse still, they are often beliefs that are limiting, fear-based, struggle-based and trauma-based. Furthermore, we add to and reinforce the programming by repeating the behaviour that causes us trauma because it is all we know how to do - until our awareness changes and eventually we do know better and then we can begin to change the programme though the likes of counselling, healing work, self-development and awareness work and Cognitive Behavioural Therapy.

There is a huge amount of information out there about this concept, a lot of self-help methods on 'thinking positively' and the Law of Attraction. I believe there might be a missing link there as what some sources of information can neglect to mention is that it isn't always as simple as just thinking in a new way or suddenly realising that we hold an outdated and false belief about an aspect of our lives. If there have been years and years of reinforcement of a particular way of living, it takes a lot more than our positive thoughts to change it. There are layers and layers of thoughts, behaviours, pains, traumas, body ailments and emotions to get through before real change is possible. Picture it like an onion, once you take away each layer, eventually you get to the core, but it takes a lot of time and a lot of tears. We face so many harsh truths, realisations, old hurts, guilt, and fear and family issues before we can even begin to input a new programme.

So, when I heard about this workshop, I didn't really know any of this. I had a romantic idea that I would go along, do a little bit of healing work and be 'healed', as they say. I can only laugh compassionately at that now. I was desperate for something to help me, a magic wand that would make all this pain and disaster go away. I decided to go for just one day. It was a last-chance saloon for me I guess, going it on my own hadn't worked so far and this was my final hope.

It started at 10am. I always like to be early for everything, so I arrived at 9.30am. The recommendation to experience Ger's work was so glowing that I trusted it and walked into the room with as much confidence as I could muster. The room was huge, it was part of the University buildings so was old and shabby because of it. There was a circle of chairs in the center, and there were six or seven people already seated. Ger was already there, looking through his CD's to find some songs to play. He was tall, with long curly auburn hair and he looked up at me when I sat down and smiled. He had a kind face, which settled me a bit and he looked like someone I could talk to, caring, down to earth and decent.

He began the day by asking us to close our eyes and he played three or maybe four songs. I'd never heard this type of music before, there was chanting and words about Spirit and Love and things I knew nothing about. I began to feel really uncomfortable; I couldn't sit still or keep my eyes closed. I was impatient and irritated by the time second song was over. 'What's the point of all this' I wondered. 'This is just wasting time, I just want to tell him what my problems are, get the answers and fix all this.'

Then, to my horror, a woman got up to dance, right there in the middle of the circle, on her own with her eyes closed and with bare feet. I wanted the ground to open up and swallow me whole right there and then. She looked about fifty-something, short grey hair and wore lots of floaty colourful clothes items with chunky beaded necklaces and things. She danced with her arms held up to the sky and spun in circles while I tried to keep my attention focused on a bit of chewing gum I saw on the floor. She better not ask me get up and dance. The expression on her face was one of either extreme pain or extreme bliss and it made me feel worse that I couldn't work out which.

'Moondancers…I've landed in with the Moondancers'…was all I could think. I thought she was a hippy, a weirdo who needed proper fitting jeans and a nice pair of heels to sort her out.

'God what have I done? I'm in hippy-heaven…Any unicorns about the place yet?' God get me out of here.

I started tapping my feet to distract me from my thoughts, desperate to be out of there, shocked by the damning and unfair judgements I found myself having of these innocent people. I was confused by why it all made me feel so incredibly angry and critical, why I was so resistant to this. I've never wanted to leave somewhere in my life as much as I did there in that moment.

Just as I was about to get up and run for my life, if my six-inch heels would have let me, the music stopped. What a relief, now we can all speak and be normal, I thought. What followed though instead, was Silence. A long, drawn out, silence. Everyone but me with their eyes closed, some crying quietly, some smiling. I just stared out the window, dying a little more inside with every second.

Ger began to speak, he asked me to introduce myself and say a few words about what had made me want to come along. I had no idea what to say, so I sat with my arms and legs crossed and mumbled something about wanting help for depression and getting over a lot of old pain and made sure I didn't meet his eye. What I did notice though, was that his voice sounded so reassuring, so gentle and so understanding, that it eased my anxiety somewhat.

The other participants where clearly well seasoned workshop attendees I thought. They each spoke at length about their deep pains, traumas and seemed to have amazing insights about themselves and spirituality that were way out of my reach.

Ger began to explain the work to me a little and I could understand it. It didn't feel at all if it was fancy notions pulled out of the sky, it felt grounded and real. It made sense to me that traumas could build up in our systems and have long-term impacts. He explained to me that there is a thing called 'Universal Energy' - a life force that creates and runs through all things and that we can call on for help and healing. It is not religious in any way, it is nature. The idea is that we can work with this energy to instigate healing in our bodies by recognising the pain, acknowledging it, expressing it, releasing it and replacing it with love. It sounded really powerful. He gave some examples of the types of traumas that people had attended his workshops for – namely bullying, addictions, abuse of all types and a feeling that the life you had built around you was falling apart.

OK...I could relate to this...This I could understand. Something in me shifted, something softened. Maybe I wasn't in the wrong place after all. I began to share things about how my life had been and the things I had been involved in. I shared more than I ever thought I could in a short space of time, it just felt safe to do so and before I knew it the words were tumbling out of my mouth.

What happened next was very unexpected. My body began to shake a little as I let the words come. I could feel my doubt begin to melt away and a massive lump of emotion build up in my throat. I told him everything, about every time my ex had hit me, about all the drinking and men and the lap dancing, the anxiety and harming myself, the bullying, about how I cried nearly everyday and thought I'd rather be dead than live like this.

My honesty shocked me but he never took his eyes from mine, he never interrupted or lost focus. He listened to every single word with the whole of his being. The pure, unconditional compassion that flowed from him was like nothing I had ever experienced and it felt so good. It was incredibly significant to me that Ger was a man and that I was trusting him enough to be so vulnerable in front of him the very first time I had ever met him. Up to that point, I had been feeling no trust or positive regard for any man outside of my family circle at all. As far as I was concerned most men were what I might describe as 'let-downs'. Ger helped me to begin to heal that; he showed me that there are men out there who genuinely care, who don't take advantage, who have good hearts and a strong integrity. I can't do the impact of that justice with words.

As I continued to talk, a huge well of emotion rose from my

feet right up to my heart. It was like nothing I had ever felt before; deep, deep pain that I didn't know my body could even contain came rushing out. Initially I tried to fight it back, to resist it, but it was too powerful. It felt so incredibly good to allow it - almost like being in a Womb, protected and loved all around.

I heard Ger say 'Just let it come.' As I went to my knees curled up in a ball on the floor. I rocked back and forth, burying my head to muffle some of the sounds I was making. I was howling like some kind of animal, loudly and unashamedly. I cried and I cried and I cried. I lay on that floor for at least twenty minutes, nobody said a word, but I was aware they had been passing me tissues and had formed a smaller circle around me while someone put a blanket over me. I couldn't stop, nor did I want to try. This felt like a breakthrough. Here I was, sobbing in front of all the people I had judged so harshly just hours earlier, and it felt great.

So this is what it feels like, I thought, to feel something bigger at work, something moving through me offering me healing and holding me in a beautiful space, these waves of heat and love and safety and release. This must be what it's all about, I felt so alive, so full, so much relief. I had cried like a child on the floor and I had never felt so God Damn free.

I sat up against a chair and I looked at Ger. He simply said;

'Anna, it's OK, keeping all that pain inside you for years must have been so, so difficult, it's OK to start to let it out, you don't have to hold it anymore.'

Maybe it was the conviction with which he said it, or maybe it was that it was a man saying it and he was acknowledging and recognising some of the pain I had felt at the hands of other men, but it felt like a beautiful healing bullet that went straight into my heart and began to heal it. I don't know why it was that day and that workshop and that moment that ignited the change - maybe it was just the right time for me, my heart opened to the possibility that I didn't have to be in all that pain anymore and that I did deserve to be heard and respected. I began to love myself.

That was the day my life began to change around. A cathartic occurrence. For the first time, I felt I was taking action to help myself instead of hurting myself. Something visceral had finally been unblocked, or unlocked, or both. The plug was put into the socket, so to speak. I was in shock the rest of the workshop, and in the closing hour, when the songs came on, I got up and I danced, on my own, in my bare feet with my eyes closed and I lifted my arms up to the sky and I laughed and I laughed, partly for the pure joy of it and partly at myself, for being such a hypocrite earlier that day and judging the others who had done the same.

To this day, Ger Lyons, remains one of my oldest and dearest friends, I trust him with my life and I consider him family. The work he did and continues to do around the world helps thousands of people. It's extremely rare to meet a man who walks in service every second of every day, so full of wisdom, knowledge, humility, integrity and a love for humankind so pure that it would humble even the hardest of people. He doesn't do the work; he 'is' the work. A Druid from the south of Ireland, he is filled with ancient and ancestoral knowledge, ripe with ceremonial and ritual teachings, he has travelled the world to learn of other cultures and has a heart the size of a Lion. He has the purest intentions to be of assistance and to help people to transform their lives out of suffering and into joy. Many, many, people's lives have changed for the better because of his work. He is deeply loved and revered throughout the world.

Thank God he has a wicked sense of humour too, although, his jokes need a lot of work, so when you meet him don't let him begin with 'Did you hear about the Irish man who walked into a bar?' Just run away if that happens.

I couldn't have been happier at that time, it finally felt as if I turned a corner and that I was moving forward. I knew I had a long way to go but it was a start and that was an immense relief. I began to research cellular trauma memory and it intrigued me. It felt like a piece of the puzzle that had been missing in my understanding of how I could begin to heal my wounds and improve my life. I grew to understand that it is actually a biological fact that trauma impacts our cells and alters them, therefore, shaping our behaviours, perceptions and health.

Once I had information and experience of this type of work, I felt empowered at last. I felt my transformation was in my own hands, I felt I was getting control of my life back and that I could become stronger. I knew I could never leave the past behind as if it hadn't happened, and nor did I want to, but I felt I could learn from it, grow, transform and move forward. There was a spark within me that had been set alight and I wanted it to burn brighter. I wanted to learn more and dive into the depths of myself and of the world of transformation, counselling and healing. I couldn't get enough of it, I felt alive and positive for the first time in many years.

I still had so much learn and I wanted to learn as much as I could. I found that socialising as I had done previously no longer interested me, my group of friends changed and I made new ones, I ate better, alcohol didn't interest me and I was determined to get formal qualifications in the counselling field that would eventually allow me to be of service to others. It wasn't an overnight solution or a magic pill, it took time and a lot of deep personal work, sometimes I reverted to old habits before I would come back stronger, pushing ahead towards my goal of getting qualified. It would still be a few years before that process began but I knew in my heart that my life had changed and that was more than enough for me. I did continue to attend some of Ger's workshops in the couple of years that followed and I continued to work on my own healing journey and transformation.

Learning Nuggets:

I believe that whether we are aware of it or not, every experience we have impacts on our mind, body and soul in one way or another. The old saying 'You are free to choose, but you are not free from the consequence of your choice' comes to mind. I learned a great deal in this period of time about how the long-term results of our choices can show up later in life, even when we think we have by-passed them or escaped them. For that reason, I'm extremely careful now about what experiences I choose to have, as I know that they will live in my body for some time to come. Discernment is my new favourite word when it comes to my choices. We all have the capacity to heal and grow; I do believe that our body and soul knows what to do to repair itself, if we just give it a chance.

I learned that men are not the enemy and that they are just as beautiful and pure hearted as my female friends and role models. Learning to love myself meant I had to learn to love men too, as I believe wholeheartedly now that they are just as deserving of love and respect as women are. Once I embraced that concept, things turned around for me. I was able to let go of years of anger, hurt, unforgiveness and pain towards the opposite sex. My life improved dramatically once I saw men as no different from women in the heart of matters and took them into my life as friends and comrades, instead of being at war with them.

As Lady Bird Johnson so beautifully put it:

"Where flowers bloom, so does hope."

CHAPTER 7 - A COUNSELLOR'S GRIEF

*D*uring the time that I was going to workshops and working on healing myself, I was building my confidence and love for life again in a different way. I had an incredible passion for Salsa dancing and I got good enough to become a teacher. By 2003 I was twenty-two and I was teaching a few days a week around Northern Ireland. Salsa dancing helped me so much in lots of ways – I was meeting new and interesting people, I was socialising in a way that didn't involve alcohol and I was exercising a lot so I felt really fit and healthy. My self-esteem was at an all-time high because I had found something that I was genuinely good at and when I danced, I felt like I was transported to another world of exotic fun and expression that was good for my soul.

After years of seeing myself as useless, being able to teach others changed my life around then. I found I was proud of myself and that was a new feeling for me. There was a great sense of community among the Salsa dancers in Belfast at that time, it was still a relatively new dance to many of us, so there was a huge interest in it and classes were always full to the brim, sometimes with seventy people showing up for a one-hour class. There were a few teachers at that time in Northern Ireland and we all knew each other. We worked towards the same goal of bringing as many people together as we could to learn and we had real fun together – meeting up a few times a week and training, challenging each other to learn new moves and organising events around Belfast.

Although it's a very different story now in 2018 as the amount of dancers and the quality of dancing has improved so much, in 2003 myself and my dance partner were among the few people who danced acrobatic moves in Belfast. This meant he would lift me up off the floor entirely mid-move and put me on his shoulders or spin me around mid-air, ending in some dramatic pose that really wowed a crowd. We designed our own moves and were self-taught so it did cause a bit of an excited stir in the Salsa scene at the time. We became quite well known for it. Apart from falling flat on my back a few times, we rarely made mistakes and we were asked by numerous establishments around Northern Ireland to attend events and do dance demonstrations, to do shows, to run Salsa nights for them and to teach classes in their venues. Before I knew it, we were out dancing and working five nights a week. I was thriving and loving the feeling of succeeding at something, it was much needed after so long of feeling bad about myself. It was the first time in my life I walked into a room and people looked at me in a way that told me they respected me, admired my abilities, trusted my opinions on dance-related things and asked for my help for them to learn. I noticed I walked taller and had a real sense of achievement about my life.

When I danced, I felt like I had found something inside myself that had been missing all along, an expression of my personality that had found an outlet at last. My self-doubt about my looks began to melt away. Salsa is a very sensual dance and for me to do it well, I had to be able to tap into my sexuality and have the confidence to express it. This felt totally different from doing lap dancing, Salsa brought out an elegance and subtlety of sexuality in me that gave me an inner glow of confidence I had never experienced. Things were looking up.

I was asked to appear on a TV show, not as a dancer but as a teacher. My job was to help a few dancers who were competing on the show to tap into their sensual side when they were dancing as the producers felt they were afraid to open up that side of themselves and that it was affecting their chances in the competition. The film crew came along and filmed me, and some other teachers, teaching a little about Salsa and sensuality when dancing. I don't know how it happened, but in the midst of discussions, I flippantly mentioned the words 'Lap dancing' to the film crew. Before I knew what was happening, I had agreed to do a mock lap dance for my friend and for the contestants to copy with their partners to help them tap into the sexual side of themselves.

In the blink of an eye, and before I really thought through the consequences, there were a number of us doing mock dances, fully clothed and laughing the whole way through it of course, nothing that couldn't be shown on TV. I knew I had got swept away with the moment and the excitement of being asked to be on TV and I regretted opening myself up in that way. I desperately hoped they wouldn't show that part of the day on the show and that they would stick to the part where we had simply done some Salsa moves and talked. A thousand thoughts and emotions ran through me for months while I was waiting for the show to be aired. Mostly, it was utter fear that I was going to be broadcast on national TV as a lap dancer after I had gone to such lengths to hide it at the time. I was furious with myself for getting carried away and terrified of what my family and friends would say if it was aired that way. I was scared I had ruined all the hard work I had done to build myself up.

Some months later, the night arrived when that episode of the show would be aired. I sat on my sofa, on my own, and watched in terror, dreading what might come. Mid way through the show, the host said 'What we have coming up next has explicit content and will be aired on another channel as part of our spin off show'. My heart began to race and I thought I was going to vomit. I flicked the channel over and waited.

It began with a song and a shot of us all walking into the venue they had filmed us at.

'So so so so Scandalous'…the song began. (Scandalous by Mis-

Teeq). Oh My Goodness. I couldn't breathe.

A voice began talking over the footage of me dancing on my friends lap, I can't remember the exact words that were said but it was something along the lines of how they had sourced a lap dancer from Belfast who was willing to be filmed helping some of the contestants to get into their sensual side etc etc. I nearly passed out with shock, regret, dread and fear. I knew that everyone I knew would be watching the show as it was so popular and, I also knew my parents watched it. I sat with my head in my hands as my phone beeped constantly with messages from everyone who had seen it, calling me a dark horse and asking why I'd never told them and similar things. The last thing I remember is looking up through my fingers covering my eyes and seeing a big red 'EXPLICIT' stamp being put on the TV screen over our faces.

I don't think I have ever felt so exposed in my whole life and it was all my own fault for getting carried away and not thinking it through properly. The show was aired all over the UK and was watched by a few hundred thousand people every Saturday night. I thought that everything I had done to heal my life had been wiped out in one TV episode. Now everyone would know, including my family. I didn't know how I would face it.

As it happened, with each person I received a message from, I saw nothing derogatory, nothing degrading me, nothing criticising me. There was a Salsa night on the following day so I took the bull by the horns and decided to go and face the music. I was pleasantly surprised by how it had been received. - There were jokes about it, shock around it and some bemused faces but not the damning judgements I had been expecting. Nobody was there to mock me or beat me with imaginary sticks for having done it. In fact, when I arrived at the venue, a crowd of my friends turned to meet me and began singing Tina Turner's 'Private Dancer', but I could see there was no malice in it, there was only surprise and jovial fun.

A good response came from my family too, they didn't judge, condemn or banish me in the way I had feared they would, they were shocked but didn't see me as any less of a person for it.

I realised, the judgements towards me were only coming mostly from me. I realised that I still had a lot of forgiveness I needed towards myself, a lot of self-love I needed to grow, a lot of old negative self-image I needed to let go of. It was a big turning point for me in accepting my past and what I had done in my life. It sparked off a huge healing for me around the guilt I felt for the things I had done in my life and also around sexuality. That event around the TV show shone light on what issues I was still carrying so that I could heal them. I doubt there could have been anything quite as effective as national TV exposure of my lap dancing to bring all those issues to my attention for healing. Thankfully, those were the years before social media existed. Yes, it came out on TV and in a way I really hadn't agreed to but couldn't legally dispute, but there was no other exposure of it, no videos shared, no pictures, no opportunity for backlash from strangers. I think if it had happened today, in this day and age, it would be a very different story for me. I would be wide open to a different type of exposure. I do feel very deeply for people now who do things that are then available for the world and his wife to watch on their phones. One mistake or slip of judgement lasts forever on the internet. I'm a huge advocate of educating the younger generations of the dangers of social media and the selfie culture. Lives, careers and futures can be ruined instantly by videos, pictures and comments that are shared. That is a thought that I never had when I was young, I didn't need to think that way, and things could be kept more private and would be forgotten about a lot quicker too then. The pressure to appear perfect that our new social media culture cultivates for our young ones worries me and I do wonder where it will end.

It was obvious to me that if I wanted to move forward in my life and use my experiences to help others, that I had a lot of work to do on how I felt about myself and my past. I would need to come to a place of understanding, compassion and love for myself. I would need to see that I had been doing the best I could under the circumstances of what I was dealing with inside. If I was judging myself this harshly, how could I be a counsellor for someone without judging them in the same way? If I had no compassion for myself, how could I have it for another? How could I really hold a healing space for someone if I couldn't even do it for myself?

That was the first time I realised what the saying 'You have to love yourself first before you can love another' actually meant for me. It was a huge wake-up call that came just before I was about to embark on my studies of counselling so it came just in time. I began my counselling studies at home in 2005. I started with a basic counselling introduction correspondence course that I could do at home and a Diploma in Psychotherapy with the same course provider. Once I had those under my belt I completed an Alcohol and Drug Awareness Certificate, an Anger Management Certificate and a Stress Management Diploma. Doing them at home certainly made it manageable and achievable for me and showed me that I had the ability to do it!

While these courses were invaluable and did indeed give me a certain level of qualification and credibility, I felt I needed higher ones to feel confident to practice and I wanted to go into a classroom environment for the additional learning, social aspect and possible placement opportunities.

In 2006 when I was twenty-five, I stopped teaching Salsa, as I wanted to concentrate on my upcoming studies. I joined a college and signed up for a part-time Higher Diploma in Counselling (with an added unit of Cognitive Behaviour Therapy) and a part-time Diploma in Gestalt Therapy. Both courses were one night a week so I was able to work at the same time as study. I was working as a part-time Care Worker in nursing homes, looking after the residents and doing arranging activities for them, whilst also going to college two nights a week as well.

I felt like I was thriving on the learning that was now in my life every day. I adored learning all about Person-Centred Counselling, Cognitive Behavioural Therapy, Jung and Freud and the like. I had a special interest in Carl R Rogers who wrote 'On becoming a Person' and in Gerard Egan who wrote "The Skilled Helper."

"Man's Search For Meaning" by Viktor E Frankl touched me deeply also, being about the suffering he observed in Auschwitz and how he and others coped (or didn't) with the experience and tried to find meaning in their lives through it. I bought countless books and I read every day to educate myself as much as I could. I felt re-born, as if I had a chance to return to my school days and have a second chance at enjoying it. One of the reasons why I loved it so much was my teacher. He was unlike any teacher I have ever had; he was unique and quirky and made it all fun whilst upholding the standards of it. He had a clear love of what he taught and he was a huge inspiration to me at that time. He really helped me to believe that I was capable of qualifying and truly helping others with what I was learning in the classroom. He encouraged, challenged and praised us all in the class and it felt to me as if I was part of a very special process of development and growth, personally and professionally. It was a very healing time for me.

With each qualification I achieved, I felt as if I was leaving another bit of my past behind me. I began to genuinely feel like I was moving forward and that I was worth more than I had believed I was. That change in my self-worth didn't only come about because I was getting 'qualified' as such – but also as I was learning more and more about counseling, I was gaining a much deeper understanding of myself through it. I had a lot of personal development and awareness work to do as part of my course and I found I was able to see just how deeply being bullied had impacted on my life and how I had played out the feelings around it for years, how I had used escape mechanisms to avoid confronting the pain I felt inside. I was finally beginning to feel a sense of self respect and value – that there was something I could give back to the world, to use my experiences and knowledge to help so that all I had been through hadn't been entirely in vain.

In my final year in 2009 I had to find a placement for my course and build up client hours. I was like a child at Christmas at the thought of getting out there into the world to practise what I was learning. I decided that I wanted to apply to do my placement in a bereavement charity called CRUSE Bereavement. I would be required to do six months of training with them and then be successful at an interview in order to be accepted. The training was beyond anything I had expected; the depth of what I was taught during that time will stay with me my whole life. It was incredibly tough emotionally; it demanded huge self-awareness and development. There was a huge amount for me to learn when it came to grief. I was faced with a large number of example scenarios that clients might present with from the death of a child, to a murdered relative, to the sudden death of a spouse and lots more. The only real life experiences I had of death were grandparents and an uncle by that stage so I knew there would be clients I would seeing whose pain I hadn't been through myself - but what I did have was compassion in bucketfuls, a lot of training and a sincere desire to be of service.

That proved to be enough and I was accepted as a volunteer. Being there I would say was by far some of the best months of my life, meeting and being present for them through their pain and grief and being able to help them through part of their process. Some of the clients I met had experienced horrific losses, things that I don't think I would survive if they occurred in my life. Mothers who had lost children in such sad circumstances, children whose parents had been murdered or were missing presumed dead, husbands whose wives had passed away beside them in bed after 50 years of marriage- a huge range of experiences of grief. I had nothing but admiration and wonder at how they got up in the morning and tried to carry on as best they could. I learned so much more about the impact of the 'Troubles' here in Northern Ireland too during that time with clients who had lost someone, maybe through a bombing, being caught in crossfire or similar circumstances. It was heartbreaking to sit with anyone who had lost someone they loved dearly in any circumstance. I could feel my heart grow and deepen and expand and I felt a real sense of responsibility working in the field of counselling. I got to see first hand how much it could genuinely help someone who just needs an ear, some hope and support. I would often leave after a day there and wish with every fibre in my being that I had been able to access that type of support when I needed it. I wished I had said that I needed it and had reached out for it. I wondered how different things would have been for me if I had.

I was soon to taste grief in a very personal way however, when I found out I was pregnant during my time volunteering in CRUSE. I'd been in a serious relationship for a year or so but I felt it was running its course just before I discovered I was pregnant. I knew something wasn't right straight away as, something within me, perhaps intuition, felt 'off.' It was two weeks after I'd had a positive test that I began bleeding. At the hospital, they told me it was too soon to tell if it was a miscarriage or an ectopic pregnancy and that I had to go in every few days for blood tests to measure my hormone levels. So that's what I did – some days they said the hormone levels were up and multiplying as they should be for a normal pregnancy and some days they said they weren't. It was too early to see anything in a scan, so it was a waiting game for me.

I had desperately wanted everything to be OK, for my baby to appropriately developing in the right place and I was a nervous wreck for weeks, begging some unseen force to make sure that it would all turn out well. I hated those hospital visits, every visit felt like doomsday to me. It took six weeks to get confirmation that my pregnancy was ectopic; my baby was growing outside of my womb, in my fallopian tube. I was crushed. Beyond being consoled in any way. I went through a massive roller coaster of emotions from utter grief, to guilt, to anger, to denial, to panic. I thought my body had let my baby down, I felt I had failed. I had a life growing inside me and it couldn't stay. The hospital told me that I would have to come back in a few days and take tablets that would basically abort the baby. I sat in utter shock and horror when they told me that. I simply couldn't imagine doing it. Of course, I knew the baby couldn't and wouldn't survive no matter what I did, but I just couldn't accept that I would have to do that. They told me that it would save my fallopian tube if I took the tablets and that I then wouldn't have to have the tube removed. They did warn me of the signs to look out for to tell if my fallopian tube had ruptured and if that happened, I would need urgent medical attention and it would be removed. I had to come back in if I felt pain in my pelvis and/or in my shoulder tips. Shoulder tip pain is a sign of an ectopic pregnancy beginning to rupture and cause internal bleeding and can potentially be a life or death situation for a woman if urgent medical attention isn't sought.

I sat in my car and I cried and cried. It felt like the worst thing that could have happened to me, just as I was getting strong, doing well, feeling like my life was moving forward this was happening. My heart was broken in two and I was silently wishing the doctors were wrong and that when I went back in, they would discover all was well and that they had made an awful mistake. I had never felt grief or sadness like what I felt in that hospital car park.

As I reached some kind of acceptance that my pregnancy was going to come to an end, I drove my car to a local cafe and ordered a coffee and sandwich. I had silently quietly spoken to the baby inside of me, and I did consider it a baby even though it wasn't what they called 'viable.' I had silently said that it was ok for him/her to let go now and that I would always love them, even though he/she never got a chance to grow and I never got to hold the baby in my arms. I was half way through eating it when I felt something in my pelvis area burst. My shoulder tips went on fire and the pain through my body was quite unbearable. I got back in the car and drove straight back to the hospital. It was too late, they said, my fallopian tube had ruptured and I needed immediate surgery to remove it or else I would die from internal bleeding. I was in too much pain and shock to feel sadness or grief at that point. A fear of death kicked in and I just wanted to get the surgery done. They had me in surgery in fifteen minutes and I woke up an hour or so later, in agony from surgery but relieved to be ok. I felt intense grief then for the loss of my baby and the loss of my body part. I felt butchered and scared. I couldn't walk due to stitches and couldn't even go to the bathroom myself without help. It was mortifying and didn't help the grieving process. A few days later when I was ready to leave, the nurses told me that I had an option to 'take the remains home.' By remains, I assumed they meant the baby, even though he/she would have been no bigger than a peanut by that stage. The nurse explained that sometimes people like to do their own little burial ceremony at home and that it can help. I readily agreed and thought it would be a good idea. I had great support from my family, the father of the baby was absent and didn't take much involvement, so I wanted to do a little ritual of my own, maybe asking my sister to join me for support.

I saw the nurse walk back over towards me across the ward with a transparent container in her hand. I nearly passed out when she handed it to me. Inside the container was my fallopian tube, floating in clear water for the entire ward to see. I looked at her in utter disbelief…that was not what I had been expecting and I did not want to carry home my own body part in what looked like a plastic Tupperware container. I think I went into shock, wondering if this was normal practice or indeed, 'best practice.' I stared at it for what felt like eternity, totally convinced I was having a bad dream. With a shaking hand, I gave it back to her and cried the whole way home when my dad came to pick me up.

It dawned on me in the weeks and months that followed – I was experiencing all the 'Stages Of Grief' I had learned about from my studies from Elizabeth Kubler-Ross.

Elizabeth Kubler-Ross was an American-Swiss psychiatrist, a pioneer in near death studies, and she wrote a widely known book titled 'On Death and Dying'. In her book she states that,

"The 5 stages of grief – denial, anger, bargaining, depression and acceptance are part of the framework that makes up our learning to live with loss and that help us to frame and identify what we may be feeling." (5 stages of Grief by Elizabeth Kubler-Ross and David Kessler).

I had known them and learned them but I had never felt them as intensely as that day. I was living what I had been studying and I suddenly understood that a book can teach the words and theory of something but it can't teach or provide experience. I thought of a few clients who had experienced losses during pregnancy and I actually felt guilty that I had been the one trying to support them, when I didn't really have enough life experience of loss and grief.

The depth of sorrow I was feeling was humbling me and I realised very quickly that while I knew a lot in theory, I had lacked the life experience of a poignant loss and I felt that fact had limited what I had been able to bring into my counselling journey with them. I felt somehow that I had lacked something that they may have needed because I was caught up in my head at times, in the theory and learning of it – trying to do my best for them and doing the best I knew how to do – but I hadn't lived it, so I felt I still had a lot to learn in terms of life experience when it came to grief. I knew how much more of my heart and soul I would have been able to bring into the counselling room if I had known fully then what that depth of grief felt like.

I was growing and developing as a person in those six years, between 2003 and 2009. I had faced two big lessons during that time – one about the need for self-love and where judgements can really come from and the other about grief and loss and how it deepens our humanity and capacity to love others and to really be present for them during a grieving process. I had fulfilled my goal of becoming a qualified counsellor and I had been presented opportunities to heal myself on even deeper levels along the way. I was grateful for that, because I wanted to grow and become the best version of myself I could be, I wanted to reach my potential and I wanted to be the best counsellor I could possibly be. I knew that would involve a huge amount of personal healing work and that life would bring me situations that would show me what still needed work within me. I saw it as 'On the job training.' I still had a few personal lessons and a lot of learning about different types of healing work to get through before I would feel ready to really be of service to others. I had a curiosity around Spirituality and some of the healing modalities that existed within it and I felt drawn to learn what I could about that field so I could deepen my knowledge and my practice. I believed that there was more to the field of counselling than I had seen so far and that there was more to us as human beings than what we had been taught. I wanted to explore more unconventional methods of healing and self-help, so the next part of my learning began.

Learning Nuggets:

Learning to love and respect our pasts and ourselves is incredibly important to our growth and happiness. I have learned that no matter what we have been through or done, we can use those times and how we overcame them to help others who are experiencing something similar. I used to wonder how I would ever see past my own past and feel good about myself again – taking the lessons from it all and using them to strengthen my own sense of self meant that they fuelled my desire to be of service to others.

Life is fragile and invaluable; my ectopic pregnancy has shown me that. Death and grief are such huge parts of our lives and the ability to face them with humility and compassion is such a gift to others and ourselves. My counselling studies have taught me that we are complex human beings with a huge capacity for love in the face of loss. Courage is what got me through - that, and a sincere hope that at the end of the day, what we all want is to help each other to heal and grow.

To finish with two Elizabeth Kubler-Ross quotes that sum up this part of my journey for me:

"The ultimate lesson all of us have to learn is unconditional love, which includes not only others but ourselves as well."

"The most beautiful people we have known are those who have known defeat, known suffering, known struggle, known loss and found their way out of the depths. These persons have an appreciation, sensitivity and an understanding of life that fills them with compassion, gentleness and a deep loving concern. Beautiful people do not just happen."

CHAPTER 8 – LEARNING TO LOVE

J had a strong desire to explore and understand more about the spiritual practices I had heard of over the years. I knew from my family stories that people in my ancestral line had experienced connections with something more than everyday skin and bone, so I did have a certain belief in the possibility of there being something to tap into. I wasn't sure what it was that I was trying to connect to or how to do it, but I had a grounded approach to the whole subject - being perfectly aware that not everything I was reading or hearing about was 'real'. I wanted to find out what was real and what wasn't. I couldn't believe something just because I read it, or someone said it. I needed to *experience* it and be able to prove, to myself at least, that I was having a genuine experience with substance to it.

I believed, and still do, that the essence of spirituality is having an open heart – not necessarily one that is free from pain, anger, fear or unforgiveness – but one that is aware of these crosses that we carry and that we try to work through for our benefit and the benefit of others too. I wasn't in that place yet and, at times, still held onto my pain as if it were a shield to use to protect myself from perceived potential hurts.

I knew that my heart was still somewhat closed, especially to romantic love. I had lived my life, to date, in what felt like a state of fight or flight all too often and, as a result, I was protective of myself and not particularly open to letting myself be vulnerable in a relationship. I found that when it came to relationships, I always had one invisible foot out the door, ready to run at a moment's notice, yet secretly hoping it would be my the relationship that saved me. Learning how to be a counsellor was certainly educating me about life and myself, but I knew I still had a long way to go before I was truly open and able to love others or myself fully. I had layers of protection around myself that were quite obvious in relationships. Although I really did want love in my life, I also pushed it away when my vulnerability was exposed out of fear and anger around previous experiences, not least my experience of Intimate Partner Relationship violence. There was a part of me that needed to remain in control, not of the other person, but of the depth, which I would allow myself to love before I ran away out of fear of rejection.

I very much desired change and growth but my mind and my old conditioning would get in the way. It would, in that case, take something pretty amazing and life-changing to alter my normal patterns. It would take something powerful enough to break down all my walls, to shatter all my perceptions of how a relationship should look and to leave me no other choice but to love, to open me up. It would take for me to be broken down to my bare bones and built up again in a new way for me to be ready to really love in all forms. Something inside me knew that I would have to love with all that I had and to lose the control I employed around my emotions in order to fully let my heart be opened. I also knew that in order to be open to what I thought might be on offer through spiritual teachings, my heart couldn't be closed and angry and protective. I was only half living and not fully loving – myself or anyone else – and that wasn't enough for me anymore. I wanted to feel what it felt like to really love. And that's exactly what I got.

I can't give you exact time frames, or identifying events or descriptions, for the same reasons I couldn't when I wrote my chapter on Intimate Relationship Partnership Violence. The best I can do is tell you it was a brief period of time between 2012 and 2016. Who the man was is not relevant to the point of my story and not naming him will not detract from my message. I will say that the relationship turned me from a girl into a woman and that there was a huge amount of transformation through it. I wouldn't change it for the world, I wouldn't be who I am today if it hadn't happened – for that I'm always grateful.

When we met it was like an electrical current of energy ran around and between us. I had never felt anything like it before, as if the space between us that joined us had a life of its own and was coursing its way through our bodies, running right through any road blocks on its way. It didn't stop or ease or have any mercy, it kept us awake at night, and it was hard for our bodies to contain it. It was so much more than sexual chemistry; it was an indescribable feeling of being connected in a blissful state of heightened awareness. It was love felt so deeply and intensely that it made us cry and shake and feel so incredibly alive that we might burst into flames. It was knowing each other's thoughts, emotions, dreams and hearts – as deeply and intimately, as we knew our own.

And that was just standing beside each other, not even touching. We knew when we were thinking about each other, we knew exactly what those thoughts were. We knew what the other was doing, when we weren't even communicating. We both started to have what felt like spiritual experiences because of the depth of emotion we felt for each other – there was something about it that felt 'divine'. We dreamt about each other sometimes, seeing deeply into each other's lives and experiences in the past and present that we hadn't shared verbally. It seemed as if we had a type of second sight that developed through our connection - we were able to see more and deeper than we could without each other. It was as if somehow, the love between us opened us both up to a deeper insight and understanding of the world, the universe, and truths about love, human nature and the like. I could describe it as feeling as if one's whole existence and understanding of life was being stretched and expanded past what either of us had ever known or experienced before. It amazed and shocked us both.

For the first time in my life I felt I really loved a man, no matter the circumstances or the outcome. I developed compassion and understanding I didn't even know I was capable of. The nature of my love for him was stretching the muscles of my heart beyond its normal capacity and I was slowly learning what it really meant to love someone unconditionally. I would hear myself speak words I'd never spoken, understand things I had never understood before about life and love and give more of myself than I knew even existed of me. Although I had sensed it would take something like this to break down my walls, I didn't seek it out. It had arrived out of the blue, taking me by surprise and no matter how hard I fought it, the love persisted and kept on smashing through all my barriers of protection until there was nothing of me but the raw and real Anna, heart in hand. It was the first time I ever felt I was a 'Soul', that there was more to me and to life than the black and white and grey tones I had been coloured in. I felt so incredibly alive, the world was vibrant, my heart was really and truly feeling intensely and I was watching myself transform from an angry and hurt girl who wouldn't let love in to a woman who loved gracefully, fully and with such gusto.

At the same time, I was coming across the concepts of Twin Flames. The Internet was full of articles, websites and discussion forums on the topic and I came encountered them as I was looking for some kind of explanation for what I was feeling and experiencing. By definition, a Twin Flame is someone who is said to be our divine counterpart, the 'other half' of our soul, our perfect mirror. They are said to be a catalyst for your spiritual growth and a reflection of your deepest beauty and strengths, but also of your shadows and unhealed parts. In essence, it is said that a Twin Flame arrives in your life to bring enormous emotional, psychological and spiritual growth. Furthermore, they are more than a romantic partner, the relationship is said to have a much larger purpose and to be about working together to bring this energy of healing out into world. This belief appears to spring from the concept of 'Twin Flames' in Plato's "The Symposium" dialogue, which indicated that humans originally had two faces, four arms and legs and that we were once so powerful that Zeus split us in half in case we should overpower the Gods. A 'Twin Flame' in that case, is the other half of ourselves that we were split from and that we are destined to meet again to become whole once more.

The criteria of such a connection is said to be a feeling of inexplicable connection and recognition to this person, being able to truly be yourself, a feeling of expansion around them, transformation of both people through the learning in the relationship, being finely tuned into their energy, you mirror each other perfectly, a magnetic pull to them, being able to be fully truthful with each other and feeling driven towards a higher purpose.

Dr Rebecca Housel has written a great deal about Twin Flames and it is worth quoting her here:

"Twins are two separate people who share no DNA, typically

come from different backgrounds, different geographic locations, and different theological backgrounds, yet "find" each other through some invisible cord." "An initial Twin Flame meeting isn't like a first date either. It's intense, electric. The kind of thing where you connect and six hours later, you realize one of you may have to go to work at some point. There's none of the awkward early relationship stuff either. You just know each other. Like you've known one another for thousands of years."

"Twin Flames have only unconditional or real love between them. You feel joy and peace together. It's like breathing for the first time. Things just feel right between you, even if you have other social obligations."—(www.rebeccahousel.com)

This relationship appeared to fit those criteria at first and yes - I bought into the concept at the start – that this man must be my one and only mirror, my ultimate love, my divine counterpart. The concept of twin flames was relatively new to me, so I tended to believe it and I held onto it for grim death. I read every article I could find; I watched every video that I believed existed on the topic. It had been the first time in my life that I had felt love so deeply and unconditionally that I was terrified of losing it. However - losing it was exactly what was going to happen and had to happen in order for me to heal the issues that it brought up to the surface in me. The abandonment I feared, the rejection I imagined might come – deep shadows began to surface once the initial high was calming down and I could see very clearly what the purpose of this connection was. I needed to heal these deep issues and I had a sinking feeling and an acceptance that I wouldn't be doing that with him around. I knew that in order to heal a fear of abandonment and rejection, that I would appear to be abandoned and rejected by him.

You see, what I didn't mention was that he was unavailable – not in the conventional sense of the word, he simply couldn't be in a long-term relationship due to various and very serious work commitments – and his work was his life, it was a huge part of his identity as a man. After months of the most intense, life changing and world-view altering contact, it had to come to an end. He had work to go and do, people he couldn't let down and priorities that took precedence over a personal relationship. After weeks of pained talks, tears, both of us trying to find a way – he sat down in front of me and he looked me straight in the eyes and he simply said, "I am never going to be able to be with you, not in the way that you want."

His words hit me like a tidal wave of shock, I actually felt them as a physical force, hitting me on my body and washing over me like water. I knew I had to believe them but it took a long time to really let that happen inside myself after it happened on the outside. Simply put, I had lived with the hope of a happy ending every day with every breath I had in my body and I felt broken when it ended.

I believed that I had no chance of ever being happy with a man again if it wasn't him. I had given him all of me, really given all of me. Heart, mind, body and soul. Every last drop of me. And we both realised it was never going to be and that it wasn't the 'Twin flame' romance I had read about and convinced myself it was. If you have ever felt that, you will know how hard it is to let go. I had never loved like that. My understanding of life and love as I thought I knew them, was broken. There was no fairytale ending, no magical reunion. Initially, I didn't want to accept that it was possible to love each other so much and open up so deeply yet end up without that person in my life in a way that followed the normal patterns of connections.

I didn't know it at the time, but he was teaching me about priorities, responsibilities and about the different things some people need for their happiness and contentment. In putting himself and what he needed first, he was teaching me what it really meant to love yourself regardless of what someone else might want from you. It wasn't that he didn't love me; it was that he would have had to give up too many of the building blocks that made him who he was in order to be with me. It would have ended up with him resenting me and feeling as if he had lost important parts of himself. I had to accept I had spent a lot of time convincing myself that it would end up being like the magical Twin Flame relationships that I had read about and it clearly wouldn't be. I began to see that buried under my protective layers was a girl who felt less than whole and that I thought I required my other 'half' to become so. I was holding him ransom and I knew I had to let that go, but it was hard.

I spent too long stuck there in that space. Too long not living, of not loving anyone but him. Too long sitting in an imaginary waiting room for him. Many nights of hoping and days of crying. Too long being angry at him for not being with me, angry at the world, angry at the commercialised concept of Twin Flames that I felt trapped me into an idea that eventually we would be together so I shouldn't really give up. I felt like a prisoner to my ideals and I knew if I didn't expand my understanding of relationships and connections that I would be stuck in a space of lack.

Every ounce of me knew that this relationship had come into my life to show me all my fears around love, around being alone, around feeling as if I had been abandoned, around not being 'enough' for someone to choose me as well as teaching me all about loving both him and myself unconditionally. It seemed remarkably unfair that I loved him so deeply yet it wasn't to be and I felt that the universe was having some kind of sick joke with me. I thought I had been through enough, thank you very much. This relationship was indeed a perfect mirror for me, just not in the way I had hoped. I did realise at some point in the midst of the madness that it was the perfect thing for me to go through to finally heal. I just didn't like it; it was so painful and bitter sweet.

So, what did I do? What was I supposed to do? I had no choice really - I had to begin to learn to love and heal myself at this deeper level. The only way out is in, I decided. Once I accepted that, I realised I would have to let go of the hope that he would one day turn up at my door like a knight in shining armour to save me from my pain. I had to make this healing process about me and only me. I had to give myself the gift of putting my happiness first, just as he had done for himself.

For me, the love remains and will always be there, but in a way that causes me no pain or regret, only gratitude and peace. The truth is, I don't know for sure if Twin Flames are 'real' or not. I wish I did, but I don't. That doesn't take away from the love and the lessons we shared and how I grew and continue to grow as a woman through my own experience. I have reached a place of understanding that some love is eternal yet free and without structure, condition, expectation or obligation. I've learned, that sometimes, love just exists above and beyond normal templates and that it is perfect as it is, it doesn't have to be pushed down, cut off or disallowed – it just needs to be accepted and enjoyed for what it is, an unconditional love for another human being with whom I have shared a part of my life with and learned so much from.

The lessons I have gained through this experience have served me well and have helped me to open up to more love in my life now, so I will always be happy it happened. Without that experience, I doubt I would be who I am today or that I would understand love and human nature in the ways I now do. It took a long time for me to see that I thought being 'chosen' by a man meant I had worth as a woman and even longer to realise that those two things aren't related at all.

In essence, this man choosing other priorities over our relationship taught me, eventually, to truly love myself.

Furthermore, once I moved through the feeling of rejection, he taught how to love, honour and respect people for choosing what they need for their happiness, even if it doesn't include me. And, to make matters even more challenging, I knew that in order for me to find real peace with this experience, that I would have to love him for, and in spite of, his decision. Otherwise, I would live in anger and blame - and I didn't want that. I guess that's what I meant when I said at the beginning of this chapter that this experience turned me from a girl into a woman.

I had nowhere to turn – but inwards. So, inwards was where I began and that is what started me on my journey towards exploring the spiritual practices I had heard about. I believed that if I could explore these healing modalities and find something that helped me to repair years of self-doubt in relation to men and love, then I was onto a winner. The formal counselling qualifications I gained and the personal counselling work I had undertaken alongside that had assisted me so much in my intellectual understanding of myself and I had grown so much from it, but this experience had shown me where I still carried unhealed parts of me that I wanted to let go of once and for all.

That was when I found out about Shamanic Practises. I was already learning a little about how to do Angel Card readings and I was delving into the world of all things Psychic and I loved it, but my learnings there weren't bringing me healing as such, it was more information that I was gathering and I wasn't necessarily delving deep into my soul to search for transformation. As I began

COMING OUT OF THE DARK

to move in the circles of people who practised spiritual readings and healings, I was introduced to the idea of Shamanic Soul Retrievals. Shamanism is an ancient healing tradition, a way to connect with all of creation and with nature. The word 'shamanism' is used widely to describe ancient practises originating with indigenous tribes worldwide. A Shamanic healer is someone who moves into an altered state of consciousness to gain access to different realms for the purposes of bringing back healing and information for the growth of the soul of the person they are working with. A Soul retrieval works on the idea that when a person experiences a trauma of any kind, a fragment of their soul can get left there, leaving the person feeling lost, un-whole, not quite themselves and often physically ill for a long time. This is called Soul Loss and it is widely believed in Shamanic circles that soul loss can be a cause of illness and dis-ease and that therefore, returning the soul part brings the client back to wholeness emotionally and wellness physically. During a Soul Retrieval session, the Shaman will travel with their own personal spirit team, which may include their ancestors and spirit animal helpers, to locate the missing soul part in the lower, middle or upper worlds. They will then enter into a relationship of sorts with the soul parts, bringing them back to the owner for healing and integration.

That is a simplistic and basic description and not one that goes into great detail or explanation of the vast beauty of Shamanism, but it is enough for the purposes of this story. So, I requested a Soul Retrieval session from a practitioner I knew because I was aware I had experienced quite a number of traumas that could have resulted in soul loss at different times of my life and I was really keen to give this a shot.

I lay down on a table and the practitioner explained the process to me and asked me to simply remain relaxed, open-minded to what I may see in my mind's eye and aware of any feelings that may surface throughout the one-hour session. She didn't ask me anything about my past or events that occurred that brought me there to see her. She began to drum and then sat down beside me after fifteen minutes and I took a deep breath. I was incredibly relaxed and as the minutes went by, memories began to float into my consciousness. It appeared to me like a time-line of events, moving from the present day backwards into childhood. I saw memories of the supposed 'Twin Flame' relationship, times that I had been crying alone and feeling lost. Moving backwards into my ectopic pregnancy and the surgery I had, I could see my body on the operating table and the shock it went through when a piece of it was removed.

Then, the images moved backwards again into the violent relationship I was in and it was as if I was watching myself from the outside, being physically hit and my body going into shock. After that, I could see myself in the bars, drinking and damaging my body, abusing it with an overload of alcohol and cigarettes. I saw myself being attacked when I was seventeen; I saw my drink being spiked and my whole system going into shock. Next, I was eight years old and back in the classroom again being bullied. I watched in my mind's eye as I could see my smaller self, shrinking in fear and rejection and hurt. I finally understood where this deep fear of abandonment and rejection came from that seemed to run as a constant undercurrent in my life. I understood why I had made the choices I had and how I hadn't known that I was really just looking to repair my inner child who was hurt and alone. I had been trying to do that for years, I realised, without knowing it from looking for validation in men, to trying to understand it through counselling, to using alcohol and sex. All the time, I had just been trying to repair an original wound that had salt rubbed in it over and over again through the years.

I felt a huge swell of emotion rising in me and my body began to shake a little, it was as if I was being shown where it had all started, where I had lost parts of myself along the way and how I had been living a sort of half-life, with bits of me missing. I felt so much compassion towards myself all of a sudden, a gentle and tender feeling of wanting to hug myself and comfort myself as a child and an adult too. I felt no blame towards myself anymore for how my life had been. I don't mean I blamed others or took no responsibility for my actions, but I was able to see the reasons why my life had went the way it did and I got back in touch with my innocence again. I forgave myself for the pain I put myself through and I forgave others too for their part in those stories. I realised – this is what it felt like to love myself.

I felt the Shamanic practitioner starting to stand up and she came over to my head and blew gently onto my forehead and onto my stomach. This is part of the integration process of them bringing the soul parts back and putting them back into your body again. I can only describe the feeling as one of coming home to myself, I felt so different. I felt whole in a way I didn't know I could. I opened my eyes and I laughed and laughed with a joy and abandon that made me want to dance down the street clicking my heels. My heart was bursting with happiness and peace. She recounted for me what she had seen and felt and she had actually seen a number of the same things that I have described above, so that was further validation for me that this was real and that I was really coming home to myself at last.

Slowly but surely, after that day, I felt those traumatic events start to melt away and they no longer impacted me or hindered my life in the way they had done. I felt myself grow wings, as if I was free from my past and I could become the person I was always meant to be. It was an unusual feeling, I wasn't quite sure what to do with it at first, but I enjoyed finding out. I felt strong, present in the moment, wise and mature and at peace. That feeling has gone from strength to strength since then and I'm eternally grateful for that healing experience. I'm not perfect and I don't float around in a cloud of love and health every day, but I am me, in a way I didn't know was possible and the greatest joy of my life was being able to start to help others on their healing path too. I never thought I would reach that place; it seemed like a million light years away. I began to learn as much as I could about healing and counselling in all forms so that I could be as informed, educated and developed as was possible, in order to appropriately help and work in a professional context with people.

I took tentative steps out into the world, offering my services to people who asked for them. I began to run groups, focusing on healing and counseling and I did one to one sessions for people and I found that process, in itself, a huge learning and transformative experience. I'd like to share some of that process with you in the next chapter as there were some magical moments that amazed me, some sad and disappointing experiences, some harsh truths about being of service to others and some incredible days that made it and continue to make it all worth while.

Learning Nuggets:

All in all, that period of time showed me a number of things. Firstly, that love isn't always what we have been taught it is and that if we can open up to the idea that it can show up in many forms that may seem in conflict to our expectations, then we can learn and grow so much from it, sharing wonderful and beautiful experiences with one another. Unconditional love is something that we often speak of, but how many of us really practice it? It's easy to banter the term around, but really living it is a real achievement and for me, a landmark in our maturity and understanding of the world 'love'. Secondly, when we truly open our hearts and minds, there is so much on offer in the form of personal healing and sometimes it is the unconventional methods that can truly bring transformation when used in conjunction with traditional methods. Although, perhaps 'unconventional' isn't the right word, as a lot of healing modalities have been around for centuries before our own traditional 'counselling and psychotherapy' existed. I believe that to research these and to try and test which ones work best for us is a good way to deepen our knowledge and experience. I do believe there is more to this world than meets our eyes and being open to that idea at least could enrich our whole lives and our healing journeys.

"Nothing liberates our greatness like the desire to help, the desire to serve others" - Marianne Williamson

CHAPTER 9 – IN THE SPIRIT

Coming into my early thirties, I began to want to really explore the spiritual realms and what was on offer that might deepen my relationship with the world and myself as well as build up my armoury to work with clients in a different way. I was especially drawn towards attending my local spiritualist church and the development classes held there. I wanted to learn as much as I could about the spirit world. I was also really drawn towards Reiki as a way of helping to heal the body and balance our energy. I was expanding my circle of female friends as I was learning more and meeting new people, many of whom became beautiful friends who shared a lot of the same life experiences as me, so working in the area of healing for women was becoming very important to me.

I felt like a flower beginning to bloom in the sunlight and I was so excited about this new world that was opening up to me. I found as I was working on healing myself, that my relationships within my family were improving too. I felt able to open up and talk to them about who I was becoming and why they were noticing changes in me. I was able to share some of my experiences with them and connect with them in new ways. This was especially true of my relationship with my Mum, as I discovered that she was interested in hearing all about the spiritual realms. I regretted the time I had missed with her by not reaching out and talking to her about anything and everything. I began to talk to her a lot more about my inner self instead of hiding that part of me. As I healed my inner feminine wounds and began to really see who I was as a woman, I found I could really see similar pain in other women and connect with the feminine aspect in people around me – friends and family alike. I could see that I had been rejecting myself as a woman at times in my life, disliking who I thought I was and actions I had taken. I understood then, there was very little chance of me being able to connect to other women until I learned to love and accept myself in my womanhood.

There was a part of me that battled between wanting to learn more about the alternative side of helping others and sticking to the formal and traditional forms such as counselling and psychotherapy. I was aware that the alternative and spiritual was often discredited by people who were working in the more recognized and established helping and caring fields such as clinical psychology and psychiatry and I didn't want all my hard work in gaining my formal qualifications to be for nothing if I went down the alternative route and was mocked by my peers for doing so.

For quite some time, I separated the two and had my friends

and colleagues in both fields that knew little about the other one. I think I wasn't sure how to synch the two and if that was even possible. I felt at times that I had to choose one or the other, not because I felt one was necessarily better than the other, but simply because they seemed like two different worlds with different beliefs and methods of helping and I didn't know how to find an approach that incorporated them both. I felt in my heart that there was more to healing than working with the mind through exclusively talking therapies. I felt, and feel, that we are multi-layered as souls, with more than just our physical body to work with, so I began to read a lot about 'Transpersonal Counselling' while learning about mediumship and practising Reiki and what I was learning was that it is a holistic approach to healing, dealing with the mind, the body and the spirit. A transpersonal counsellor and their clients will view the work they do together as an opportunity for personal and spiritual development. That sounded to me exactly like the approach I wanted to take in my work. I was determined to learn as much as I could about the 'spirit' part.

Reiki

By the time I was thirty-two I had already qualified in Reiki, a Japanese form of energy healing, and was using it with family and friends or anyone who asked for some healing. I had spent three months training with a teacher in a little town outside of Belfast called Holywood and was awarded a Reiki Master qualification by the UK Reiki Federation (CNHC Registration). I discovered that I could somehow 'feel' where someone had pain in his or her body. I was intuitively guided to that area and often saw it in my mind's eye and could pinpoint the condition or issue they were having. When I put my hands above a client's body, I would feel pin pricks of pain in my palms when I was above the area of their body that they were feeling pain in. Reiki works by laying your hands on or just above the client's body and is based on the idea that we all have a universal life force energy that flows through us and can be channelled with the intention of offering healing. It is said to balance the client's energy system, clear energy blocks and promote relaxation. I have carried out hundreds of Reiki sessions to date and have always found the client has felt benefits from it.

In saying that, I always worked with a physical problem that the client was currently experiencing at the time of seeing me or the residue of something they had experienced in the past and still experienced flare-ups. I never, ever predicted or foretold of an illness to come and would not have wanted to be shown or to know of them. I have seen the damage and trauma it can cause to someone when they go to a 'healer' and are told they have some physical condition on the horizon. Firstly, in my experience, the healer can very often be wrong and cause unnecessary worry and even if they are correct, it can scare the client beyond belief. If I had a client come to me for Reiki and asked me to predict anything to do with their health, I refused. It simply felt too risky and potentially disastrous should I be wrong.

I remember one client, in particular, who had no belief in Reiki or anything 'alternative' when it came to helping herself. She had been bought a gift voucher to come and see me and was quite reluctant and tense when she arrived. As she lay down on my table she told me she didn't even want to close her eyes during the session, as she felt so uncomfortable. I thought it was a good sign that she was willing to at least try it and we began the healing session. After ten minutes or so, I noticed that her eyes were beginning to close and that her body was relaxing. I was beginning to sense that her heart was in a lot of emotional pain and my hands were burning when I held them above that area. About half way through the session, she began to cry – gently at first and then real heart felt sobbing. She lay like that for another twenty minutes and then sat upright on the table and really opened up to me about what was happening for her in her life.

She was going through a marriage break-up and all her hopes and dreams were shattered. She told me it was the first time she had felt able to talk about it and that she was amazed at the energy she had felt moving through her body while receiving Reiki. She said she had seen colours and felt a heat coursing through her body, relaxing her nerves and helping her to open up. We spoke at length after the session and she went on her way home, looking radiant and relieved of a heavy burden from her shoulders. Around three months later, she called back in to see me and told me that she had felt so amazed by her experiences during her session that she had just signed up to become a Reiki practitioner herself and that she felt a whole new world had opened up for her. She looked incredible and her energy was beautiful and peaceful. It's because of experiences like this that I have so much faith in the alternative side of healing; to see how my client transformed and began her healing journey was a privilege to be a part of.

Spiritualist Church

The first time I ever went to a Spiritualist Church in my early thirties I was attending a development group for beginners and we were being taught to connect with the Spirit World, to bring through messages of love and support from loved ones who had passed away. Spiritualism is based on the belief that each of us is a Soul, residing within a human body and that once our body dies, we live on in the spirit world as a soul retaining memory and personality from when we were here. It follows then, that a 'medium' knows or learns how to tune into the energy vibration of the soul and receive messages to pass on to the client.

Although I knew a little about mediumship growing up and hearing the stories about my relations, I didn't feel I had ever really been able to tune in or feel anything much and if I had ever tried on my own, I wasn't in a position to find out if I was right or just imagining things as there was no client or willing volunteer to try it out with.

When I walked into the spiritualist church I was extremely excited and also very nervous. I wasn't afraid of mediumship or the idea of a spirit, I had just always naturally assumed it was real; it felt like the truth to me since I was very young. My nervousness was more centred around whether I would be able to make a connection or not, my uncertainty of what it would feel like if it did happen and if I would correctly interpret it or not.

We sat in a circle and the teacher played some beautiful music that sounded like a thousand angels were singing all at once. I felt myself begin to look around the room and see who else was there, if I knew anyone, what age groups came to this sort of group and to try and help myself feel comfortable. Everyone looked incredibly normal, just like me. I wondered how many times we walked down the street past people and didn't know that they were capable of communicating with our loved ones who have passed away. I sat quietly, very excited about what might happen and feeling that somehow, I was at home here.

We were guided by the teacher to close our eyes and bring our attention inwards, to feel our breath moving in and out of our bodies. After a few minutes, she talked us through a relaxation exercise where we were to imagine white light rising from our feet, slowly up our legs and through every part of our body. I noticed I felt incredibly relaxed and peaceful. I felt myself smile in the silence. Our teacher then guided us to imagine expanding our energy out beyond the confines of our bodies and up towards the ceiling. She asked us to internally and silently ask for someone from the spirit world to step forward into our space and to make themselves known to us.

I felt my stomach jump a little at this point, unsure of what I was supposed to be feeling or noticing happening. After a few moments, my heart began to speed up, as if I was exercising, even though I was sitting completely still. I felt my breath quicken and my palms get sweaty. I felt as if I was a little dizzy and off balance for a few seconds and as if somehow my body wasn't made of skin and bone anymore, but energy in motion instead.

Then the best bit happened, pictures began to flash in my mind of a young man and he was playing football. I could see him very clearly but only for a few seconds at a time. His facial features were quite detailed to me and little distinctive characteristics were apparent. It was as if I was remembering something I had seen years ago, but he wasn't someone I knew or had ever met. I felt a strange sensation in my stomach area, as if butterflies were moving around. I began to feel what I can only describe as phantom pains in my back and I instinctively knew that this young man had fallen during a football match and damaged his back. In my mind's eye, I saw an outline of a man's body and some of the areas of his body were coloured red, as if drawn in with a colouring pencil. I've since learned that for me, that means that the person in question had problems with that part of their body and perhaps passed away due to those issues and when I relay that information, it is validation for the recipient that I am indeed communicating with their loved one.

At this point, the teacher asked if anyone felt they had a connection with someone from the spirit world and if so, we were to stand up and relay the information we felt we were getting. With my hands shaking, I stood up and began to speak. I blurted out everything that I had felt and seen without looking at anyone to see if he was recognised. I was worried I was making a complete fool of myself and imagining things, so I had to get up and speak quickly in case I got too scared and didn't do it. As I finished speaking, I looked up slowly and saw a lady in the circle raise her hand. She said that she recognised the young man as her cousin and that everything I had said about him was true. I was, to say the least, delighted and was genuinely in shock that I had experienced something so vivid and real and had been able to sense and interpret the information that was coming through. I could see from the lady's face that it meant a lot to her that her cousin had come to say 'hello' and that was the best bit of the whole experience for me. I gained an understanding of the gift of mediumship and the responsibility that comes along with it. I think I became aware really early on in my journey of mediumship that it was essential to stay grounded with it, to remember that it isn't about sensationalism or glory for the medium. Rather, I understood that it's a beautiful healing experience for the person in receipt of the message and can bring so much joy, peace, comfort and love. I had a healthy respect for it from the start and if anything, was in awe of it and wanted to learn more.

Over the next year or so I went to as many groups and classes as I could, wanting to develop and become better at mediumship. I had some fantastic teachers along the way who really helped me to understand my own style and how the spirit world worked with me. There were many times that I lost confidence in myself and felt as if my ability to connect had vanished. Normally, that was when I had some of my own healing needs to attend to first before I could go deeper on my mediumship journey. I found that when I was changing or working on my own life, when I had moved through it my mediumship grew and got better. I got clearer messages, descriptions, names and personal 'clinchers' as I call them – little phrases or memories that I see and relay that only my client and the person communicating with me would know. I wanted to be really good at it, not for attention or validation for myself, but because I had seen the positive impact on people of getting really clear and indisputable messages from people they loved who had passed away. I deeply desired to help in that way if I could. I didn't always get it right and, sometimes, I disappointed clients by being a bit off the mark with the information I felt, but I always tried my best and sometimes, there were magical moments that shocked even me – moments that made it all utterly worthwhile and brought me to tears.

One such moment was when I got some information in a reading about a part of my client's car that I was being shown needed to be fixed. I could distinctly see during the reading that there was an issue with the clutch, nothing dangerous but a problem nonetheless. I mentioned it and left it at that. A beautiful lady I felt was her mother came in close beside me and after relaying the information I was feeling about her, my client confirmed it was indeed her. She gave me very specific instructions for her daughter that I was tell her. She told me that she needed to turn down the classical music playing on her radio in her car on the way to the celebrations of her 20th anniversary. That was it.

A week later, I got a phone call from my client, who was in a state of shock. She had been driving to the anniversary gathering, playing her classical radio very loudly. She remembered the information that I had passed on from her mother and turned it down. Just a moment later, she heard a faint crunching noise coming from the car and had to pull over. The AA told her it was a problem with the clutch and that if she hadn't heard the noise when she did, her car would have been a write-off. Phone calls like that really warm my heart and deepen my faith.

Reading Cards

I was also learning a great deal about reading cards for people around this time in my early thirties. I had an interest in both Angel and Tarot Cards. I had been to a few card readers in the past myself and some had been pretty on the mark, finding insights into my past, present and future. Of course, there were some readings I went for that were totally inaccurate, but I still believed there was something to it and I wanted to access it as part of my work. The readings that I had been for and that had been on the mark had provided me with so much clarity and insight that I was sure there was truth in the idea that readings could access information that wouldn't normally be available to our logical minds. In the beginning, I didn't really understand how it worked or what it meant to read a card. I would look at a card and take the literal meaning from the description and apply it as gospel. I saw a lot of disappointed faces from clients when I did that and I wondered what on earth I was doing wrong. I marvelled at the readers who seemed to be able to take a card and develop their reading from it, make it personal to the client, pick up or somehow know information beyond it. I wanted to learn how to do that.

I visited a local tarot reader who I'd had a reading from and whom I trusted and I asked for her help. She sat with me for nearly a whole day, teaching me how she does her job. She explained to me that the card is simply a tool to work with, something to help access the other information that was available. She told me how reading someone was about blending my energy with theirs and she showed me how to sit opposite her, relax my whole system and to imagine that my own energy was like a big bubble around my physical body. She asked me to take deep breaths and to imagine that with each breath I was expanding my energy outwards, to meet her bubble of energy and that the two were becoming one, blending with each other.

She told me to notice every little thing I felt during that blending. Every physical sensation, image, thought, emotional feeling and any instinctive sense of knowing about anything. I began to understand with her help that everything I was experiencing in the big bubble was information about the client and their life, emotions, physical body and the potentials for the future. I say potentials, because that's what I have come to learn about future predictions – that they are 'potentials' rather than 'certains' – and should be relayed to the client as such. We have choices in life and when faced with a crossroads and decisions, we have options to take. Depending on what we decide, it can alter the outcomes, therefore in my experience, telling a client that a particular outcome is guaranteed is a mistake and can sometimes result in disappointed clients returning asking why their situation turned out differently than the cards had shown.

The next time I was trying out a card reading with someone, I tried the technique that she had shown me. I used Doreen Virtue cards that I had bought in a local holistic shop and I liked her 'Angel Tarot' and her 'Healing With The Angels' deck. I found both the messages and the artwork on the cards very inspiring and uplifting to use. It felt totally different from what I had been used to. I was much calmer, much more centred and sure of what I was feeling and seeing. I found a lot clearer and accurate information coming with incredible details to me.

Suddenly, the penny dropped about how this stuff works. I had been trying and trying with my mind to find information on the client during a session somehow, to work it all out in my head and no wonder I hadn't been doing so well. I finally saw what I had been hearing others say. I needed to let Spirit show me the information and to trust that I would be shown what the client needed to hear or see at that time.

Spirit

What or whom do I mean by using the term 'Spirit' The term may mean different things to different people and nothing to others. I think it's a really personal choice to decide what that means to you, but for me the word Spirit refers to the 'Other World' and all that I feel that contains. I believe in 'Guardian Angels' and that angels are spiritual beings, assigned to watch over us individually or as groups of people, countries or nationalities. I believe we have spirit guides and helpers, angels and relatives who have passed over who help us. I believe they help us through our senses - giving us gut instincts, intuitive knowings, dreams, signs, visions and the like. I believe we can ask for help, guidance and direction and that we will get it, although it may not be exactly what we want to hear or see at times. I have seen through my own experiences that there is a lot of support available from the spirit world, a lot of healing and guidance that we can call on if we trust what it is we get back as an answer.

The experience that stands out for me the most was the light that appeared in my room when I was a child and going through the bullying. The sense of love and peace that washed over me was undeniable and although I did spend some difficult years wondering if Angels really existed, I always held that night in my heart and returned to the memory and feeling of it when I began to learn more about the Angelic Realm. I do get little white feathers when I ask for signs and lots of other symbols appear when I ask for guidance, be it a sign on the side of a van that catches my eye with a perfect phrase to answer my question or a quiet sense of knowing I'm being guided towards something that is for my higher good.

Connecting with Myself

I was working intensely on my own development and skills during that time and I found that I was growing, feeling very content within myself, happy to be alive and excited about the future. Looking back, I can see that period of time as a major turning point for me in how I felt about myself. I genuinely began to love being in my own skin and I really liked who I was becoming – I felt I was who I was always meant to become. Gone were the days and nights of emotional pain, guilt, regret, self-doubt and the like. I felt so good – as if I was being nourished and that I had something to give back to the world, something to contribute.

When I was thirty-five, I decided that I wanted to run some support and empowerment groups for women. I was reflecting back on all the things that had helped me to overcome my difficult experiences and realised just how much a women's group would have added to my healing journey. I knew if I had been in a group with like-minded women then I would have gathered even more support, learning and growth and I wanted to provide that for other women now that I felt I was in a totally different place within myself. I felt well equipped and with enough knowledge and experience behind me to begin something small. I wanted my groups to be a place where women could come and share their experiences with each other, share knowledge, skills and to offer support to each other. In essence, I wanted it to be a space where growth through love, acceptance and support was possible. I had been researching the idea of a women's gathering called a 'Red Tent.'

A Red Tent gathering is an ancient tradition where women would meet on the new moon when in need of support, empowerment and rest. Traditionally, girls would join when they had their first menstrual cycle and would learn from the elders about their body, fertility and all things woman-hood. There would also be an opportunity for them to learn about the different stages of the moon throughout the month and how that impacts on their emotions, bodies, productivity and creativity. It is created as a space to celebrate being a woman and all that goes with that, a time and place for reflections and healing. Red tent gatherings are centuries old and worldwide, where women from many cultures would come together once a month and share the space. I sincerely feel that our modern culture needs more of them as I see a distinct lack of gatherings and nowhere for young girls to go during through this initiation into women-hood, meaning they are often left alone and confused with mixed emotions and a lack of support.

The first Red Tent that I held was such a beautiful experience for all involved. I had gathered up lots of red flowers, cushions, blankets and candles. I set the room up and laid out some crystals, angel cards, incense, inspirational books and everyone brought some food to eat once the group was over. We began the two-hour gathering with a meditation and each person took a turn to introduce themselves and say a little about why they came. I found that each woman who spoke had a story to tell, a reason why they needed help and support at that time in their life. The openness and honesty in the room was breath taking, the tears flowed just as much as the laughter and the sense of oneness was palpable. I began to realise as the night went on that I didn't need to do anything, the group took on a life of its own and the women involved took ownership of it. It was not down to me to have a programme of activities or to plan exactly what we would do. I discovered all I needed to do was to be present, to listen, to allow it to grow organically on its own and see what the group needed and wanted it to become as the night went on.

In other words, I got out of my head and into my heart. I got out of the thinking and into the feeling. I got out of the planning and into the trusting. I began, over time, to realise that I needed to that in a lot of areas of my life, to just be present, listen and trust. I began to practise that every day and not only did I find daily life a lot more pleasant and less stressful, but I found things flowed beautifully and I was generally much happier and in my heart instead of worrying, stressing and trying to control how everything I did turned out. Life began to shift for me as I thought less and felt more.

I ran the groups for a year or so, once a month, and every time surprised me in the most beautiful ways. We had many profound experiences and many laughs too. One day in particular a group of women and myself were standing in my garden around my fire pit and we had written down our intentions for the coming month on bits of paper. We were going to throw our writings into the fire as tradition says that doing so sends the energy of your intentions out into the universe to manifest. We had drums and we were taking the whole thing very seriously. As it came to my turn, I stepped forward with paper in hand and moved towards the fire. I took one final look up into the sky to silently ask for help and as I did, a seagull flew over my head and landed a massive white splat of bird-poo on my face. We all collapsed with laughter as I squinted out of my eyes and tried to wipe it off. My belly was sore from laughing so hard and I realised how important humour is in life, how important it is to be human and to know that at any minute something funny can happen that reminds us that we are human beings, open to the normal foibles of everyday life.

I grew so much as a woman by running the groups and I made some amazing friends, women who I trust and love beyond measure. I know the groups did truly benefit the women who came along and I'm really grateful for the chance to have been a part of that. I would have continued to do them for longer, but working in the evenings became impossible for me due to family commitments – I do intend to start them up again someday soon though as I feel they are so valuable for all involved.

Kitchen Witchery

I have a particular interest in something called Kitchen Witchery. It's a type of cooking that uses the magical properties of things found in and around the home, such as herbs, essential oils, foods, spices, plants and everyday objects. Kitchen witches may use ritual and ceremony and the use of chanting, they may begin a spell of cooking by calling in the natural elements of fire, water, earth and air to assist them while they cook something intended to be used and eaten for promoting their health, increasing wealth, promoting self-love and lots more.

I was so excited to learn about this. I was aware from a young age that food has certain properties as I knew when I ate well, I felt amazing. I grasped that vitamins and minerals in food had positive impacts on our health but I was like an excited child to learn the magical properties that our ancestors knew about food. I bought every book I could find on the subject and cooked enough different recipes to feed everyone I knew for a month. The types of food I would have cooked were things such as 'Love Cookies' - cookies made with the herbs and spices known for promoting self love such as cinnamon and star anise, doing a ritual before the cooking began and calling in the elements to help build the power of the food. I made breads that contained oregano and rosemary for good luck and happiness in love and basil biscuits for abundance and increased financial flow. I found through time and experience that they worked, but only if I had a strong sense of intention as I was cooking them and had directed that intention into the food. I think that's the same for anything in life isn't it? We get out what we put in, if we have focussed intentions and a clear idea of what we want to achieve, then it's more likely to happen I believe. I read somewhere once that maybe that's what magic really is, totally focussed intention towards a desired outcome – and that it can be used for the good or the not so good. I've seen both at work and I'll stick with the good for sure.

Interestingly, I found that quite a few women were interested in learning about this topic, so we got together and held cooking days where we would learn from each other and have fun bonding through the day. There was often a little fear around the term 'witch' however. It is a term still associated with an old fashioned cliché of a woman in black robes, cooking up evil and harming others, always at risk from being burnt at the stake for her practises. I would often spend a little time at the beginning of my workshops explaining that kitchen witches are not to be feared and that there are many food, herbs, spices and the like that can be used for our better good.

Pulling the Different Strands Together

Over time, I began to learn how to incorporate my formal qualifications and training with all the alternative methods I had been learning about. It meant then that if a client came to see me with a relationship problem, for example, I could work with them on their thoughts and emotions through my counselling and psychotherapy, but that we could also look into helping them to heal their body and the impact of the stress they were feeling through Reiki and maybe some messages of support from their loved ones who had passed or some cards to offer them hope and inspiration. I found this method of helping yielded really good results for clients; it's an all-rounder so to speak, helping the mind, body and spirit.

I've continued to work like that for the last few years; pulling in whatever skills I have, depending on the clients' needs and wants. The feedback from clients is that it has helped them to reach a deeper place of healing, quicker than if they were using only one of the options on offer. I often feel that all my life experiences that led me into the learning and training I've done are now being used to benefit and help others – that is such a good feeling – to know that none of it was in vain and I have turned pain into gold.

A client of mine has been kind enough to provide me with a testimonial to use for my book.

"I've had the pleasure of knowing Anna for a number of years now and she is a truly amazing woman. Her healing knowledge is unquestionable and her accurate readings have brought me great peace of mind and comfort in difficult times. Her readings are deeply thought provoking and she has brought me wonderful messages from dearly departed and sadly missed family members that have made me both laugh and cry at the same time. Anna is also an amazing and highly qualified counsellor and her knowledge and ability combined with her wonder calm, caring and thoughtful demeanour all add to the fabulous experience of working with her along my journey" (K. Dawson)

I was deeply moved to receive this testimonial; I find sometimes that we aren't aware of how profoundly we can touch someone's life. When I read this, I realised on an even deeper level that all the hard work I've done over the years was worth it if what I offer can help someone that much. I wasn't just transforming for my own benefit, I was transforming for the benefit of others too.

Learning Nuggets:

Learning so much about the alternative side of healing was such a beneficial thing for me to do. There were lots that appealed to me and some practises that didn't do so and I simply used what worked for me to bring a holistic approach into my work. Time, experience and results with clients has shown me that there is so much more to us, as humans, than our thoughts and emotions and there is a world of help available to us in a spiritual sense, if we keep an open mind and find out what we can relate to and what feels true to us. Seeing that we are not alone in this world and that we have guides, angels and loved ones around us has brought me so much comfort and hope for the future – once I understood that we have many layers to us, I got really excited at the prospect of how much healing and growth is on offer if we can tap into what is all around us and ask for help. I think a huge number of us are growing and changing as people and beginning to open up to ideas and concepts that previous generations may have laughed at – it's an exciting time to be alive.

Many of my clients will ask me at the end of a session if I think everyone has the ability to tune into the other world of mediumship, readings and healings. I always respond in the same way – I tell them that everyone is a spiritual being, every single person here on earth is spirit incarnate and has access to the help and support available from the spirit world. I have seen so many people who never believed they could do a reading surprise themselves by how much information they can access when they realise that fact.

I would always recommend to people that they attend reputable classes in either Spiritualist Churches or with private teachers whom they trust are working with integrity and have a proven record of good readings and teachings for both mediumship and psychic reading development.

For developing mediumship, I would recommend that people attend the Arthur Findlay College, in Standsted, London. I spent a week training there and the standard of teaching is above and beyond anything else I have experienced. Many of the teachers from the college will run their own groups and classes privately and these are invaluable too.

To become a reiki practitioner, it is essential to attend the class of someone who is a registered teacher and is affiliated with the regulating body they work with. Having the necessary qualifications to practise safeguards both the client and yourself and ensures good practise.

Most importantly, spiritual development is a deeply personal journey and one that nobody can actually teach you how to do. Yes, you can certainly be taught the tools to use and be offered support throughout your development, but the real work takes place alone and internally. What I have come to learn is that the more we heal ourselves, the clearer we are as a channel for information from the other world. My favourite way to describe it is that we are like water pipes. If our pipes are clogged up with emotional and mental debris, they get blocked and the water (spirit) can't flow through at full force. It may come out as a dribble or in spurts, but it won't be free flowing and clear. Clearing out the pipes means deep personal healing of our pasts, our issues and our pains and that takes time and happens in stages, like layers of an onion – one layer at a time. I've found that with each layer of the old healed, we reach a deeper and richer place within ourselves and gain a better understanding of spirit too.

The biggest recommendation I can give to anyone wanting to develop their spirituality and their abilities to read for others is to approach it with integrity, humility, respect and as little ego as possible. Make sure you have good friends and teachers around who will help you when things get tough, keep your feet on the ground and above all – always work from your heart with the sincere desire to be of service to others. Being a reader, a medium, a healing practitioner and indeed a counsellor is not about self-glory – it's about genuinely wanting to help others through their pain and into a space of peace and self-love.

So, work on yourself, trust yourself, look deeply into your own soul and find the pain that needs healed. Face yourself and all that you fear makes you unlovable and when you find those reasons that make you think you aren't good enough, love them so intensely that they melt away and the darkness turns into light. Then, shine that light for others to see so that they can have a hand to hold while they start that scary journey for themselves. As the saying goes - 'We are all just walking each other home."

A quote to finish:

"You are a divine being, you matter, you count. You come from realms of unimaginable power and light, and you will return to those realms" - Terence McKenna

Anna Gray

CHAPTER 10 – RIGHT HERE, RIGHT NOW

Words can't express the journey I've been on writing this book. I'm so incredibly grateful for the chance to do it. I know how lucky I am to have been offered the opportunity. The support I have received from the very beginning has been breathtaking, both from my publishing company themselves and family and friends. I won't pretend it's all been plain sailing because it hasn't. Now that you've read my book, I hope you will understand why I'll say that I had real moments of panic and doubt about sharing these details of my life. The fear of judgement was huge and to say I felt exposed would be a gross understatement.

On the other hand, I chose to do it because I wanted to share a message I felt was really important, one of transformation through the darkness. I know it sounds like a cliché, but I mean it when I say that if what I have written in this book helps just one person then every word of it has been worth it. That's not to say that it hasn't helped me too because it really has. I was surprised just how much actually. I found as I was writing that I gained an even deeper understanding of myself and of the events that have happened in my life, both the challenging and the beautiful. I had plenty of 'A-Ha!!' moments and there were times that it felt as if pieces of a jigsaw were slotting into place for me. There were also times when I was writing that I was overwhelmed with emotion and I cried at the memories, the hurt, the love, the regret, the hope.

My fear of writing about the brief lap dancing and phone sex experiences was debilitating at times. I debated whether to include that part of my life in fact, up until this last chapter to be exact. My fears of what people would think of me, the stereotypes connected to it, what my family and friends would think – it overtook me at times and I often rang my sister or my partner in a total panic asking them if they thought I was mad to leave myself so wide open to potential criticism. I decided, in the end, that despite my fears about it, I had to be brutally honest if the message was going to have any real impact at all. I just couldn't dilute the truth, because then the healing and transformation message would also be diluted and that would have been such a loss.

Nothing I have ever done has ever pushed me out of my comfort zone like writing this book has and it truly has changed my life for the better. My sense of understanding and compassion for myself grew beyond measure through this process and I feel like a better and stronger woman for doing it. I battled for a long time with myself on how to write this last chapter. The mix of emotions I felt that I wasn't expecting surprised me. I had assumed I would be really excited to get my book finished and that I would write the last chapter quickly and with a clear sense of what I wanted to say. That really wasn't the case at all. I stalled and stalled until it I was nearly out of time with my editor.

You see, there was a part of me that felt like once I finished it, that would be the end of my story somehow and that maybe there would be nothing left to happen in my life. Writing a final chapter on my life seemed to scare me into feeling that maybe that meant my life was in its final chapter and that I was saying it was concluded and over. That took a while to dissipate and I can laugh at that now, knowing full well that there is so much more to come and so much that I have to look forward to as the person I am today. In a way, it is the end of one part of my life, the parts filled with pain and fear. That girl, so driven by a sense of desperation and loneliness, is long gone. I've come to love that part of me so much, instead of feeling shame and guilt and embarrassment at who I used to be, I adore it and my heart is full of nothing but compassion.

I think one of the biggest things I have learned in life is that when we can't truly be comfortable with all that we are and all that have been, when we can't stand the feeling of being in our own skin, we can never truly feel at home in the world or find our true sense of belonging and purpose. We always end up running in circles, searching for answers outside of ourselves, looking for reasons to confirm that we aren't lovable after all. When we can learn to accept every little thing about ourselves, especially what we might feel is our darkness, things can change for the better and suddenly we can start to see that we are already perfection just as we are.

I was afraid to finish this book, because I knew that once it's completed then it will be out there in the world, for real actual people to read instead of just being font and text on my computer screen. I'm not sure I thought that far ahead to be honest, as I was wrapped up in my little safe world of writing all my inner most feelings and my secrets and nobody had to know except me. The realisation that it would be out in bookshops hit me like a ton of bricks about half way through the whole project. I know it sounds silly, how could I not fully realise that before? But it was something that seemed like years away and many thousands of words away and I didn't allow myself to fully take it in. I might not have written anything if I had. The fear might have won instead.

I guess that's the thing I've hoped has come across in my book – I was swamped by fears my whole life, all types of it. Fear of being unlovable, fear of 'mistakes,' fear of men, fear of anything and everything. It was like a disease that killed my joy in life and my ability to really get to know myself because I was so afraid of what I would find if I dug deep into my soul.

My journey has certainly been one of learning to shed as much fear that I'm not really lovable as I can and knowing that it's ok that I still feel it sometimes – I just try to make it my friend and work with it, not against it. It was only when I stopped fearing fear, that I found I could transform it into something of a great healing tool for myself. Living the majority of my life with low self esteem and all that went with that meant there were emotions, experiences and landmarks that I couldn't fully enjoy because I wasn't fully present in the moment. Looking back now, I can see that a lot of my life was spent in survival mode and it deeply saddens me to think of all the magical moments I missed because I was so wrapped up with anxiety and stress. That has changed now, thank goodness. The joy I'm able to find in the little simple moments in life is astounding, be it sitting in the garden and watching nature move and flow all around me or eating a meal with my family and seeing the joy on their faces as we enjoy good food and being in each others' company.

I spent a lot of time thinking that I should be travelling the world to find the magical and transformative places and moments, when the truth for me is that I had all I needed within me, right where I was, the whole time. I found that I believed I would find more healing and growth by travelling the globe to find places, people and things outside of myself that would magically help me to understand life. There is so much to be gained through travelling and meeting people and learning. However, I was running away from where the real healing opportunities lay, within myself in my own environment with my own family. My good friend, Ger Lyons, who I wrote about earlier in my book once said something to me that changed my whole perception on this. He told me - *'If you want to help the world, start with your own self, in your own family. That's where the real workshop is – in your own daily life.'* He couldn't have been more right. I needed to stop running away from myself, searching for answers everywhere but inside. Once I did, everything changed.

With almost every single client I have worked with, no matter what issue they present with initially, I've discovered that underneath what the immediate issue is, lays the deep and buried fear that they aren't loved, aren't good enough, aren't accepted – by themselves and by others that matter to them. I don't believe I've ever met anyone who didn't feel that way at some point in their lives.

So, yes – underpinning my whole book is the theme of low self-esteem and a lack of self-worth. Living a life feeling that way is torturous. It's not a life at all really, it's a constant struggle for survival that just gets too much to cope with every now and then when the fight gets too much and our heads are barely above water gasping for air.

I couldn't continue trying to live that way, something had to give. I didn't want that something to be my hope and my will to live. I wanted to thrive in the waves of life, flowing with the ups and downs and knowing I am my own anchor, that I didn't have to drown. I still have moments in time when I doubt myself and times when I don't feel good, but the difference now is that I have a strong foundation of self-love to fall back on. These days, when I feel fears and doubts about myself or about life in general, I know I have the ability to help myself back into a place of strength and happiness. I know there is help available - from myself, from family and friends and from the other world of angels and guides who only offer us unconditional love and support. I've had some amazing help along the way as you know from reading this book, but nobody could walk through the door for me. I had to take that leap myself.

What does that mean then, to take that leap? I'm sitting right now writing this and I'm listening to a song by Sinead O'Connor called 'Healing Room'. It's a beautiful song of hers and my favourite by far. She sings about how the healing room resides inside of us, not on the outside. When I first heard it, it really struck a cord with me in terms of how I tended to look outside of myself for answers over the years and that I didn't fully understand that the power to bring healing to myself, was inside me all along. I looked outside for approval, validation, acceptance and love – when really what I needed to do was to give those things to myself. I was putting my faith and trust in everyone else's opinion of me and gave very little attention to building up my own self-love.

'Taking the leap' for me, meant taking the risk to actually really examine myself, to look deep into every corner of who I am – especially the dark and dusty ones that I felt I wanted to avoid. Writing this book brought that to a whole new level for me, I had no choice but to excavate my truth and face myself in a full length mirror, shadows and light. I do believe that we can't fully love who we are until we love our darkness too - all the bits of us that we try so hard to cover up and hide – the selfishness, the greed, the betrayal we are capable of, the desire to control, the lust for power – to mention a few. I've come to learn that human nature is neither black nor white; it's shades of grey. We can be all the wonderful things and all the seemingly ugly things at the same time and that's what makes us real and lovable humans. I found when I was afraid of parts of myself that I thought made me unlovable that that's when my self-esteem spiralled lower and my self-destructive tenancies took hold. There is immense freedom and peace to be found in just being ourselves as it's exhausting and draining to pretend to be anyone else. When we deny our shadow side it has a tendency to take over as we try to deny it, fight it or change it.

I believe we all have parts of ourselves that we are ashamed of and would love to eradicate and keep in the dark. However, I have found when we bring it out into the light and admit when we feel low, insecure, jealous, greedy, venomous and the like, we can accept that we are multi-faceted human beings with a huge range of emotions and aspects that make us who we are. Then suddenly, our shadow side loses its' power over us and no longer feels like such a threat to our worthiness as lovable people. We stop needing to run away from parts of ourselves and our pasts that make us feel ashamed. We feel we can integrate all parts of ourselves into the whole person that we truly are in our souls. It's ok not to be someone else's idea of perfect, or indeed our own idea of perfect. We are true perfection just as we are; there is nothing wrong with us. We are all just learning how to be here in this school called earth.

Life is good for me these days, it's been a long and difficult journey to come home to myself but one that I believe my soul chose on some level for the purposes of growth, learning, transformation and healing – to gain a deeper understanding of the meaning of love in all it's forms. If we can learn to see life as a series of lessons we are presented with for growth, things suddenly don't seem so scary. There is no deadline we have to meet that if we don't meet it, we've failed. We have time; we have endless opportunities to learn and re-learn and unconditional love and support along the way. We are loved, just as we are. For me in my life now, there is nothing more important than love, be it for family, friends or myself. I haven't come across a problem that can't be helped with more love.

You will have noticed throughout my book that I didn't appear to be 'lucky in love' as the term goes. It's true – there were a few turbulent relationships and too many times my heart felt like it was shattered. I repeated what may have looked like mistakes after mistakes to the outside eye, appearing to never be successful in forming a stable, committed and happy relationship. I couldn't count the number of times I said 'Here we go again' to myself when another relationship broke down that had felt so full of hope and promise. I was utterly convinced that I was destined to be alone and that there was something fundamentally wrong with my ability to relate in a way that was sustainable and fulfilling on all levels. I held a traditional view that the only marker of relationship success was to get married, have kids, get a mortgage, settle down, work for years and enjoy grandchildren one day. There is nothing wrong with that picture at all. That can be exactly what a successful relationship looks like for some people, if that's actually what they truly want. I know lots of people who have that and they are some of the happiest people I know. However, in my past, I believed that I HAD to follow that plan as if it were the only template that was acceptable. With that in mind, I had often felt like a failure for not achieving that happy family picture. I tried to create it and it didn't work for me because my heart wasn't in it, I was playing out someone else's ideas, something I had been taught by society along the way. I was living to some else's conditions.

Once I let go of that idea and accepted that every relationship was a success because I had grown through it, I realised that I didn't need to try to force myself into a picture that someone else had painted. I began to view relationships differently and see the beauty in every experience. Once I was happy and content to be alone if that's what I needed to be at that time, I stopped chasing the idea of being saved and rescued by some fantasy of an ideal set up. I became so content to be by myself and yet so open to love at the same time.

In my heart, I always held a sacred image of the type of relationship that I wanted - loving, honest, real, evolving, conscious, fun, passionate, spontaneous, rock solid and full of expression. I was often told that those types of relationships don't exist and that I should simply settle for less or spend my life alone and searching.

The thing is, they do exist, but only if we have that type of relationship with ourselves first. How on earth can we expect to have a wonderful deep and fulfilling relationship with another person, when we don't relate to ourselves in the same way to begin with. If we don't love ourselves, if we aren't honest with ourselves and if we don't evolve within our own selves, how can we possibly hope to share that with another person? I understand now where I went wrong in the past, although it wasn't *wrong* as such; it was more a learning curve. I was only connecting with people in the ways and to the levels I was connecting to myself – and that wasn't always in a deep and authentic way. I truly believe we can only have the type of relationship with another that we have with ourselves and that expecting it to be any other way is a recipe for emotional pain and repeated negative behavioural patterns.

Once my relationship with myself changed, how I related to others changed to mirror that automatically without having to try. Once I got real with myself and gave myself all the qualities that I wanted from a relationship – then and only then did how I relate romantically and otherwise begin to change and a whole different type of intimacy happened. The saying is true, it really does start with loving ourselves first and then our relationships change naturally, they have to.

It was then and only then, that I entered into the relationship that is all the things I dreamed my ideal relationship would be. I'm not talking about a fairy tale fantasy of love where two people meet and there is nothing but idealistic highs and no challenges and we both sail off into the sunset to life of perfection. I'm talking about realness, honesty, overcoming obstacles, genuine love and care for each other, vulnerability and rawness. I'm talking about holding each other's hands through the storms, not avoiding them. I've been lucky enough to enter into a relationship that is truly intimate, that acknowledges the light and the dark within us both and loves all the parts regardless. The difference is I entered into that relationship feeling 'already whole' and not searching for someone to fulfill me. I have grown so much as a woman because of it and it has immeasurable value to me. It's ironic that the minute I let go of the idea of a happy family picture and decided that it wasn't for me, that someone came along who showed me what it really meant to want that and to choose it. He has taught me the beauty of commitment, family, understanding, settling down, of loving someone with all my heart and of letting myself be truly loved. The one thing I always believed wasn't meant for me has turned out to be the one thing that has enriched my life beyond measure. My gratitude for him is beyond words on a page.

I have learned so much about counselling, psychotherapy and the formal routes of helping others. I've also delved quite deeply into the alternative side of healing and the spiritual aspect of life. I have educated myself as much as I possibly can so far and I'm not done yet. However, there has been no greater teacher to me than human relationships. I can read a thousand books and go to a million workshops, but nothing comes close to the learning that comes from everyday living and loving through human connection. I've seen nothing in my life that will trigger us like a close relationship, nothing that will show us what unresolved pain we still hold within us as barriers to letting love in fully. I've seen nothing that will touch us so deeply and help us to heal like trying to move into deeper intimacy with our loved ones and dealing with all that brings up in us from our childhoods and beyond.

The main message of my book, through all my stories and disclosures, is that I believe that a lack of self-love and a feeling that we are not good enough is the root cause of a huge amount of our internal and external discord. I believe that change is possible and that growth and transformation happens when we allow it and welcome it. I never would have believed while I was burying my pain in a drink, a toxic relationship or any situation where I behaved like I was less than loved, that one day I would be writing a book talking about it all. I never believed I would be able to help others with similar problems, I never believed one day I would be working in the fields of counselling and healing, I never believed I would feel happiness and peace – but I do. It is possible to evolve, to let go of pain and to grow into the best possible version of yourself. It takes courage and it's not easy, but it is possible. That image you have in your heart and mind of you at your happiest and best – you can achieve it. Believe it.

I wish we were taught to care for and love ourselves as quickly as we are taught subjects in school. I believe that part of the purpose of life is to learn to love, ourselves and others, and that each painful and difficult experience we have is an opportunity to do so. We can take that opportunity or we can leave it. If we leave it, the painful emotions have a tendency to keep returning in cycles, until we make the choice to face them and work through them. If we take it, it may be difficult and challenging, but the healing and transformation that comes is invaluable. Taking the leap into self-discovery is worth it.

There are five main ideals I swear by now and they underpin how I live my life and what I try to teach through my work:

- The only person that can make you happy is yourself – you have everything you need inside of you to heal, grow, evolve, learn and love.
- You must love yourself before you can truly know how to love another person - There is no way around that, no short cuts, no cheats. It starts with you.
- Your fear of not being good enough is at the heart of the majority of your unhappiness – once you realise how wonderful and lovable you really are, all else falls into place by itself.
- Fear will strangle your joy – there is a huge amount of freedom and growth to be found in pushing through your fear. There is help available if we only ask, from fellow human beings and

from the spirit world.

- Whatever the problem, love is the way to fix it – learning to give ourselves and others more love can transform pain into pure gold.

Thank you so much for reading my story, I have really enjoyed telling it and I hope with all my heart that it gave you some inspiration, information, hope or healing of some form through the reading of it. I know I have learned a very great deal through this process and gained so much more insight into myself and the world around me whilst writing it.

I know my story is far from over as this book is my life up to now, but there is so much more to come. I know I have so much more to do and I'm motivated by my desire to be of service to others who are experiencing pain and a feeling of disconnection from themselves and the world around them. In my work with clients, there is very little I haven't heard, very little I haven't tried to help with. It is my purpose in life to continue to help, in a non-judgemental and compassionate way. No matter what I went through, being able to use what I learned from those experiences to help others makes the hard work worth it. I adore my work, my clients teach me just as much as they learn from me. I'm constantly surprised, often completely humbled and incredibly grateful for the trust that they place in me with their innermost emotions and processes. Nothing brings me more joy than to watch somebody transform and find peace and healing.

It was important for me to address both the formal route of counselling and psychotherapy and the alternative route of spirituality. I do believe in a holistic approach to healing, I do believe in things that others may not or may discredit and that's ok. We don't all need to believe in the same things to accept one another as human beings. For me, the important thing is looking into each other's hearts and remembering that we are lovable; we are worth compassion and understanding. We are human, we make mistakes and we have the right to learn and grow from them. We deserve to feel safe and secure, basic human needs are not a luxury, they are a necessity. We are worthy. We all have some kind of gift to contribute to the world. We are all unique, there is only one of each of us – let's not waste our uniqueness by comparing ourselves or competing with each other.

We are already whole.

I'd like to end my book with a poem I wrote when I was first considering writing my book and battling with my fears around it. It was a breakthrough moment for me and my hope is that it helps you to break through that any fear you might have that is holding you back from following your dreams right now:

The Fight

He grips my neck like a vice, his long dirty fingernails scratching at my apple-blossom skin, strangling the sweet nectar of truth that sits wedged in my throat.

"I'M BACK" he sneers...with his face pressed close to mine and the smell of rotten animal carcass on his breath. Oh how I had dreaded his return!

"Let me go!!!!"...I plead with him..."You've had your dirty way with me too many times before...!!" Salty tears escaped from my wide and frozen eyes, wetting his muddied hands.

But he grants me no mercy and instead, he laughs, his yellow bitter spittle splashing on my cheeks. I can feel my belly rise, my panic hanging in the Forest air like mist on Hallows Eve.

I see the Beetles gather at my feet, waiting for my timely death, so they may feed on my maiden flesh. I pause...and wonder if I should fight...use all my will to throw off his crusty blackened hands from me.

His breath quickens, as he looks me in the eye, his Power glints and flashes like lightening in a Paris storm. I'm fading now, as his grip tightens and the Forest darkens. I can hear him, laughing at my weakness and his arousal at my impending defeat is clear.

The grass beneath my naked form is wet, the frantic sweat and tears, seeping into Mother Earth, begging for reprieve, for just one more breath, one more chance to find a flicker of my soul, of my strength, before my ripped and bloodied chest heaves for one last time...leaving me a hardened mass of skin and matted hair on the Forest floor.

"PLEASE!!!"...I beg him...whispering this time..."Please go!!..." But with every word I speak, he sucks from me my dignity to feed his twisted soul.

"That's it..." I tell myself as I let my breath come to a stop, as my strength to fight him disappears into the trees. "I give in. Do your worst...I'm not afraid of you any longer..."and I surrender to my fate as he readies himself to swallow me whole...I feel my body melt like ice into my final moments.

And in that instant, his dark eyes change, defeat spilling from them like milk from a mother's breast. His hands release their scaly grip and he is gone...as quickly as he came.

And then I finally see it...that it was only when I feared him no longer, that Fear himself gave up.

Love, Anna x

APPENDIX 1:1 MATERIAL RELEVANT TO CHAPTER

I found some articles during my ongoing research that I would like to share snippets of:

Biology of Memory and Childhood Trauma
Ann W Burgess, DNSc, FAAN, CS; Carol R Hartman, DNSc, CS; Paul T Clements, Jr, MSN, RN

- Journal of Psychosocial Nursing and Mental Health Services. 1995;33(3):16-

"In a sense, when the trauma is over, the alarm system remains somewhat stuck between the accelerated fight/ flight response and the numbing state. Now, the adaptive capacity is altered. This alteration is a cellular change that becomes fixed in its patterning and is difficult to change. Of particular importance are various theories of modulating effects in the brain. Many people understand and appreciate the fight/ flight response and numbing in the face of danger; now the fact that trauma can have a lasting effect on basic processes of adaptation and growth is beginning to be understood."

Embodied Memory, Transcendence, and Telling:
Recounting Trauma, Re-establishing the Self
Roberta Culbertson (bio)
Memory and Silence

"Naive public conceptions of memory, and the attendant assumption that memory takes certain forms and not others, contribute to a curious circumstance surrounding the victimized survivor of violence. The survivor most often, nearly invariably, becomes silent about his victimization, though the experience nevertheless in every case remains somehow fundamental to his existence, and to his unfolding or enfolded conception of himself. This silence is an internal one in which the victim attempts to suppress what is recalled (so as not to relive the victimization countless times), or finds it repressed by some part of himself which functions as a stranger, hiding self from the self's experience according to unfathomable criteria and requirements. It is external as well: the victim does not tell what she recalls, in part because others do not seem to hear what is said, partly out of a conviction that she will not be believed, and more basically because she simply cannot make the leap to words....

Yet despite this silence, the momentous nature of threats and harm to the body dictates that violence and trauma nevertheless leave the survivor preoccupied with the memory of it, which itself seems both absent and entirely too present. Most disturbingly, bits of memory, flashing like clipped pieces of film held to the light, appear unbidden and in surprising ways, as if possessed of a life independent of will or consciousness."

About the Author

Anna Gray is a qualified Counsellor and Psychotherapist and has been working with clients on a one to one and group basis for a number of years. Anna uses her professional training combined with her wide knowledge of Spiritual practises to work holistically with clients in a unique and powerful way. What makes Anna's work so special is that she walks her talk; she works from the heart and has a sincere desire to be of assistance to others. Anna has helped many people walk through the darkness and come out the other side stronger, happier and in love with life again. She is considered a genuine and down to earth woman, with vast life experience and a wealth of knowledge in her field. Anna is already working on her next book with Book Hub Publishing - a workbook - designed to provide self awareness and personal development exercises for anyone who feels the call to uncover more about who they truly are, what holds them back and and how they can fearlessley step into their authentic selves.